POLITICAL REFORM IN ISRAEL

To Yael,
"For her price is far above rubies."
(Proverbs 31:10)

Political Reform in Israel

The Quest for a Stable and Effective Government

AVRAHAM BRICHTA

sussex
ACADEMIC
PRESS

BRIGHTON • PORTLAND

2 4 6 8 10 9 7 5 3 1

First published 2001 in Great Britain by
SUSSEX ACADEMIC PRESS
PO Box 2950
Brighton BN2 5SP

and in the United States of America by
SUSSEX ACADEMIC PRESS
5824 N.E. Hassalo St.
Portland, Oregon 97213-3644

British Library Cataloguing in Publication Data
A CIP catalogue record for this book is available from the British Library.

Library of Congress Cataloging-in-Publication Data
Brichta, Avraham.
Political reform in Israel: the quest for a stable and effective government /
Avraham Brichta.
p. cm.
Includes bibliographical references and index.
ISBN 1–902210–73–5 (alk. paper)
1. Proportional representation—Israel. 2. Representative government and representation—Israel. 3. Israel—Politics and government I. Title.

JF1075.I7 B73 2001
320.95694—dc221   2001032263

Typeset and designed by G&G Editorial, Brighton
Printed by TJ International, Padstow, Cornwall
This book is printed on acid-free paper.

Contents

Tables

Foreword by Gabriel Ben-Dor

Avraham Brichta's *Political Reform in Israel* is a masterly study of the craft and art of politics. More than that, it is a model of true political sociology, which stays away from the temptation to reduce politics to the study of social origins of leaders and followers.

Instead, it concentrates on the interplay of social and political cleavages with electoral systems, in the best tradition of the classic works by Sartori and Lijphart.

This is a work of great theoretical value, and also of great practical utility. It demonstrates not only what political reforms are like in complex electoral systems, but also what they cannot do and should not be expected to do. Instead of radical ideas popular with the public, the author suggests reforms that are as modest as they are prudent and practical. All this is done with great erudition, analytical profundity and a fine eye for the details in which the devil likes to reside so much.

This is an important, instructive and highly readable book of political science. In addition to the major contributions it makes to the debate on political reform among scholars and the members of the general public, it also demonstrates qualities that are sorely lacking in that kind of debate: insight, caution and political wisdom.

Gabriel Ben-Dor
Professor of Political Science
Director, Center of National Security Studies
Past Rector, University of Haifa
Past president, Israel Political Science Association

Preface

The division of Israeli society along socioeconomic (left versus right), religious (orthodox versus secular Jews), ideological (hawks versus doves), national (Jews versus Arabs), and ethnic (Sephardic versus Ashkenazi Jews) cleavages has been the major factor in the formation of its multi-party system. The deep division of the Israeli society and its multi party system has required that its governments be based upon the principles of power sharing, namely coalition governments. Power-sharing coalitions have been based on proportional allocation of resources and offices among the coalition partners. Consequently the adoption of a proportional (PR) system has become the only option in Israel's deeply divided society. The adoption of a PR electoral system while stemming from the extreme division of the Israeli society has also been responsible, to a large extent, for safeguarding its multi-party system and even intensifying its polarization. The extreme multi-party system has thus become the major factor in making the establishment of a stable and durable coalition an arduous task, and continuous efforts have been made to reform its political system in order to achieve a more stable and effective government. Thus, Israel's quest for political stability has made it almost a perfect "laboratory" for testing the impact of reforms on the functioning of the political system. The aim of the reformers has been to reduce the number of parties in order to establish a more stable and effective government.

This book analyzes and tests the many reforms proposed and implemented in the electoral, parliamentary, and local government systems in Israel, and their impact upon the stability, effectiveness, responsiveness and representativeness of the Israeli political system.

In **chapter 1** the nature of the extreme country-wide PR list system by which Israelis elect their single-chamber parliament – the Knesset – is discussed. The main properties of the electoral system, mainly the ballot, the district size, and the electoral formula, are described and the merits and demerits of the present electoral system in the view of its supporters and its critics are analyzed.

In **chapter 2** the continued struggle to reform the present electoral system is discussed. In 1948 the Election Committee of the Provisional State Council laid down the principles of the electoral system by which the Constituent Assembly, which later became the First Knesset, would be elected. In almost all the Knessets thereafter proposals for reforming the electoral system were tabled, mostly as private members' bills. The various proposals for changing the electoral system, mainly the introduction of a simple-majority single-ballot system, various proposals for a mixed constituency country-wide PR system, and a number of proposals to increase the legal threshold, are described.

In **chapter 3** the political consequences of the proposed electoral reforms for the election of the Knesset are analyzed. The manipulative nature of electoral engineering is examined on the basis of simulations testing a large number of proposals to reduce the proportionality of the present extreme proportional representation list system, by increasing legal and effective thresholds, mainly the district magnitude and the formula for allocating seats in the Knesset (the Israeli parliament). Some of the propositions of Douglas W. Rae's pioneering study *The Political Consequences of Electoral Laws*[1] are examined, and their validity tested also, in view of Lijpharts[2] recent criticism of the flaws in Rae's analysis.

In **chapter 4** the causes of the establishment of a premier–parliamentary system, and its impact on the stability and effective functioning of the political system, are discussed. An alternative model, based on the principle of the German Kanzler System, is proposed. Until the 1980s, Israel had a rather stable and quite effective parliamentary system, with a powerful executive headed by a prime minister formally regarded as first among equals, but actually enjoying a powerful position in leading the govern- ment. In the 1990s, when the stalemate created by small and medium-size parties led to a situation of immobilization, the proposal for the direct election of the prime minister was adopted, out of many reforms proposed since the establishment of the state.

In **chapter 5** we discuss the impact of the premier–parliamentary system on the representative function of the Knesset. The data collected on one aspect of the representative passive or "mirroring" functions of the Knesset are presented. The data on the social background of the Israeli MKs (from the First Knesset elected in 1949 to the Fifteenth elected in 1999) in terms of gender, ethnic, national, religious and residential origin demonstrate that instead of strengthening the stability and effective functioning of the government as contemplated by the initiators of the new premier–parliamentary system, the reform has brought about an increase in the sectorial representation, causing extreme fractionalization in the Knesset and thus undermining the stability and effective functioning of the government.

In **chapter 6**, I discuss proposals for adopting the presidential or semi-presidential systems in Israel. The suitability of adopting the American presidential system, or the semi-presidential system established in the Fifth French Republic, in the Israeli circumstances and their possible impact in improving the stability and effective functioning of the Israeli political system are analyzed.

In **chapter 7** the political consequences of the direct election of the prime minister, on the national level, and the heads of local authorities, on the local level, are compared. An attempt is made to examine whether the new electoral system has succeeded in improving the stability and effective functioning at the local and national government levels.

In **Concluding Remarks**, I discuss some of the reasons for the failure of the various reforms proposed to change the electoral system of the Knesset, and the failure of the premier–parliamentary system to achieve the hoped for results, namely improving the stability and effective functioning of the government.

In the **Postscript**, I briefly discuss the new *Basic Law: The Government*, promulgated by the Knesset on 7 March 2001, which abolished the premier–parliamentary system, and re-established the parliamentary system according to the principles proposed by the author of this book.

It is to be hoped that the new parliamentary system, based to a large extent on the principle of the German Kanzler formula, due to take effect in the election to the Sixteenth Knesset to be held in November 2003, will improve the stability and effective functioning of the Israeli political system.

Avraham Brichta
Haifa, June 2001

Acknowledgments

Chapter 4 is an updated version of an article published in the Annals of the *American Academy of the Political and Social Science* 555, January 1998. Chapter 6 is a slightly revised version of an article, "The Proposals for Presidential Government in Israel: A Case Study in the Possibility of Institutional Transference," published in *Comparative Politics* 19, October 1986. Reprinted with permission.

I would like to express gratitude to my colleagues Yael Yishai, Gabriel Ben-Dor, Yair Zalmanovitch and Ami Pedahzur for their advice and encouragement. I am indebted to Eran Vigoda and Yosi Ben-Naim for helping with the collection of the data presented in chapter 5, and to Doron Sapir who worked on some of the simulations presented in chapter 3. Finally, the intelligent, diligent and efficient assistance of Eran Zaidise made publication of the book possible.

Political Reform in Israel

The Quest for a Stable and Effective Government

1

Main Characteristics of the Electoral System to the Knesset

Israel elects its single-chamber parliament, the Knesset, on the basis of the most extreme form of the proportional representation (PR) list system.

The Ballot

In the United States and Great Britain, the voter casts a ballot for individual candidates; in Israel, one votes for a list of candidates.[1] Any group of 2,500 eligible voters, as well as any one of the parties represented in the outgoing Knesset, may submit a list of candidates. A new party, in addition to the minimum 2,500 signatures of supporters, must make a small deposit, which is forfeited if its list is unsuccessful in being represented in the Knesset. Each list of candidates may contain up to 120 names, and the large parties do, in fact, put up this many candidates, equal to the number of Knesset seats. The actual ballot cast into the box contains only the letter representing the party; no names are inscribed on it. The voter chooses a list of candidates and may not add the names of new candidates, eliminate candidates, or change their place on the list. The Israeli citizen can vote only for the list in toto, or abstain. Israel has thus adopted the most rigid type of list system.

District size

In the Anglo-American democracies, which use the simple-majority single-ballot system, the country is divided into as many single-member constituencies as there are seats in the legislature. Even in countries using proportional representation, the country is divided into a number of multimember constituencies. Only in Israel does the whole country function as a single 120-member constituency.

The number and especially the size of the electoral districts are of great importance in determining the distribution of seats in the legislature. District magnitude is defined by the average number of members elected in a constituency.[2] As a rule, the larger the district, the more proportional the election outcomes will be – that is, each party's share of the seats will be more nearly proportional to its share of the vote. The great magnitude of its single electoral district accounts, to a large extent, for the near perfect proportionality of the electoral system in Israel.

The Electoral Formula

From the elections to the Second Knesset in 1951 until the elections to the Eighth Knesset in 1973, Israel used the most extreme proportional formula in the allocation of seats to the Knesset. The only obstacle for tiny splinter groups until the elections to the Thirteenth Knesset in June 1992 was the rule that lists obtaining less than 1 percent of the total of valid votes could not participate in the allocation of seats. After the deduction of invalidated votes and of those cast for lists obtaining less than the 1 percent threshold, the total number of valid votes was divided by the total number of seats in the Knesset; the resulting number was known as the Hare quota.[3] For instance, if a party received 409,000 votes and the quota was 10,000 that party would receive forty Knesset seats and would have a remainder of 9,000 votes.

The difficulty in using the Hare formula stems from the fact that a number of seats remain unallocated at the end of this process. Until the elections to the Eighth Knesset in 1973, Israel used the "largest-remainder" formula in allocating the remaining seats. Although the size of the "remainder" is a matter of pure chance, it has been maintained, correctly, that the largest-remainder formula favors the small parties. The number of parties participating in the allocations of seats in the Knesset has usually been more than five; each party, whether small or large, can utilize its remainder only once. It is obvious, then, that the share of the small parties in the allocation of the six or seven remaining seats will be greater than that of the large parties.

In 1972 the two largest parties in the Knesset, the Alignment and the Likud (Gahal, the Herut–Liberal bloc, in the Seventh and Eighth Knessets), joined together in an effort to change the electoral formula. They succeeded in passing a private member's bill, known as the Bader–Ofer bill, to re-institute the highest-average formula used in the elections to the First Knesset and thereafter abandoned. In spite of the small parties' tumultuous outcry against the proposed change, the bill was approved during the last session of the Seventh Knesset and the highest-average formula has been used in the allocation of seats since the election of the Eighth Knesset in 1973.

Although it is true that the highest-average formula favors the large parties – this was precisely the intention of its inventor, Victor d'Hondt – its bias in favor of the large parties in Israel has been counterbalanced by the very large size of the constituency. Thus the use of this formula in Israel, the whole country constituting one 120-member constituency, has the effect of transferring less than 5 percent of the total number of seats from the small parties to the larger parties. The net gain of the single largest party has never exceeded two seats, or less than 2 percent of the total number of seats in the Knesset (see table 1.1).[4]

Strengths and Weaknesses of the Present Electoral System[5]

In the view of its critics, Israel's present electoral system, used in the elections to the Knesset until the introduction of primaries in the 1990s, had the following shortcomings:

1   The list system made the representative almost entirely dependent on the party leaders and the party machine. Loyalty to the party leaders was of paramount importance in the representative's actions and deliberations. In the Knesset, the Member (MK) was bound by strict party discipline, and could act independently only in matters of minor importance or when the party decided to grant freedom of voting.

2   The representative, whose career was almost entirely dependent on the party leaders and machine, had no incentive to maintain close contact with the voters. The voters had no representative to whom they could appeal to solve their problems and to represent their needs and interests or to whom they could voice opinions. Thus, the electoral system prevented any meaningful communication between the representative and the represented.

3   The extreme proportional representation list system concentrated the power of nomination in the hands of a small group of party leaders, and thus tended to stress party loyalty as the main quality required of a candidate. Consequently, the recruitment of party functionaries was preferred over that of candidates having a greater capacity for independent deliberation and decision making.

4   The supporters of electoral change claim that the great increase in

Table 1.1 Allocation of seats in the Tenth throughout Fifteenth Knessets under the d'Hondt, Hare and LR formulas (in number of seats)

Party*	Knesset 10			Knesset 11			Knesset 12			Knesset 13			Knesset 14			Knesset 15		
	(1) Present Allocation d'Hondt Formula	(2) projected allocation LR–Hare	(3) Difference between 1&2	(1)	(2)	(3)	(1)	(2)	(3)	(1)	(2)	(3)	(1)	(2)	(3)	(1)	(2)	(3)
Likud	48	47	+1	41	39	+2	40	38	+2	32	32		32	31	+1	19	18	+1
Labor	47	46	+1	44	43	+1	39	37	+2	44	44		34	33	+1	26	26	
Shas				4	4		6	6		6	6		10	10		17	17	
Mafdal	6	6		4	4		5	6	−1	6	6		9	10	−1	5	5	
Aguda	4	5	−1	2	2		5	5										
Degel Hatora							2	2		4	4					5	5	
Ratz	1	2	−1	3	3		5	5		12	12		4	4		10	10	
Yachad				3	3		2	2					9	9				
Mapam							3	3										
Shinui	2	2		3	3		2	2								6	6	
Tehiya	3	3		5	5		3	4	−1									
Tsomet							2	2		8	8							
Moledet							2	2		3	3		2	3	−1			
Kach				1	2	−1												

	Knesset 10			Knesset 11			Knesset 12			Knesset 13			Knesset 14			Knesset 15		
Party*	(1) Present Allocation d'Hondt Formula	(2) projected allocation LR–Hare	(3) Difference between 1&2	(1)	(2)	(3)	(1)	(2)	(3)	(1)	(2)	(3)	(1)	(2)	(3)	(1)	(2)	(3)
Ometz				1	2	−1												
Morasha				2	2													
Telem	2	2																
Rakah	4	4		4	4		4	5	−1	3	3		5	5		3	3	
Progressive (PLP)				2	2		1	2	−1									
Democratic (DFPE)							1	1		2	2		4	4				
Tami	3	3		1	2	−1												
Haderech Hashlishit													4	4				
One Nation																2	3	−1
United Arab List																5	4	+1
Yisrael B'Aliya													7	7		6	7	−1
Balad																2	3	−1
National Bloc																4	3	+1
Merkaz																6	6	

* See Glossary.

Israel's population, from immigration and the dispersal of the population through the establishment of new settlements and development towns in various parts of the country, calls for the representation and articulation of specific regional interests in the Knesset. Only a division of the country into single or multi-member constituencies could meet these needs.

5   The present system, according to its critics, encourages the multiplicity of parties and makes it necessary to establish coalition governments. This undermines the stability and effective functioning of the system.

The supporters of the present electoral system put forward the following arguments explaining their firm opposition to any form of electoral reform.

1 *The structure of the party system*
The political parties in Israel were established as parties of principle, each with a definite ideology and a particular Weltanschauung. As Professor Akzin has pointed out, "Basically, the profusion of parties (in Israel) results from strongly ideological character which most of the parties possess and reflects the multiplicity and intensity of views which various sections of the population hold on economic, religious and other matters."[6] In addition to the function of representing various outlooks and ideologies, political parties in Israel articulate a myriad of ethnic, religious and socioeconomic interests. Therefore, the Knesset is regarded as a body of ideological spokesmen and group representatives. Since interest articulation, and aggregation, is based on national and functional considerations, the division of the country into territorial constituencies would create artificial entities.

2 *The size of the country*
In a small country like Israel, there is not room for regional representation. Moreover, the adoption of a constituency system, and particularly the division of the country into small constituencies, would bring about a preference for local interests over national interests, increase the pressure of particularistic interests and consequently damage the efforts made to accelerate the process of integration.

3 *The lack of relevance of close contacts between the representative and the represented in Israeli circumstances*
Israel is a densely populated country. Most of its inhabitants live in the coastal area, with more than one-third of the population living in the vicinity of Tel Aviv.

To claim that the interests of people living on the left side of a street in Tel Aviv are different from the interests of their neighbors on the right side of the same street verges on the absurd. Moreover, the claim that meaningful contact exists between the representative and the represented is being questioned even in countries using the single-member constituency system. Even in Britain the Member of Parliament is dependent on the party and particularly on the selection committee of the local branch, for nomination. This also explains the almost total absence of independent candidates in the British Parliament. As recent studies have shown, British voters decide to vote on the basis of issues, party platforms, and party identification, and only to a very small extent on the basis of the personality of the candidates.

4 Representativeness

The present PR system is the most effective in enabling the legislature to fulfill the "mirroring" function.[7] The PR system makes the Knesset a truly representative body and prevents a minority in the electorate from attaining a majority of seats in the Knesset.

5 Stability

The multiplicity of parties does not necessarily cause governmental instability. The stability of a political system is not to be measured by the number of parties, but by their ability to create relatively stable coalitions. The party system in Israel, between 1949 and 1977, could have been classified as a centripetal rather than a centrifugal system.[8] Since 1977, the tendency has been toward the creation of two major blocs: the Labor Alignment and the center–right (Liberal–Herut) Likud bloc. Furthermore, the rather remarkable stability of the political system in Israel, until the 1990s, has been attained under the present electoral system. Finally, when the voters decided that a realignment of the political forces was necessary, the transfer of power from the Labor Party's long-time hegemony to a Likud government did occur in 1977.

2

The Struggle for Electoral Reform

The debate over changing Israel's electoral system to the Knesset has become one of the most heated in the country's political arena since the establishment of the state. The controversial issue has been presented as a panacea for healing all the deficiencies of the present political system (in the eyes of the reformers) and as a Frankenstein that could destroy the very foundations of Israel's democratic system and the pluralistic fabric of Israeli society (in the eyes of those opposing electoral change). Those who favor reform believe that changing the present electoral system to the Knesset will bring about the establishment of a more stable government, capable of dealing efficiently with the many difficult, complex problems facing the country. Those who oppose any reform argue that manipulation of the present electoral system will result in the elimination of many political parties, which will then have no alternative but to resort to illegal activities, thus undermining the state's social and political stability. Adoption of electoral reform, it is further argued, may lead to the formation of a one-party system in which one party may attain an absolute majority in the Knesset with the support of a minority of the electorate; again, the legitimacy of the political system will be undermined. To understand this controversy the electoral system will be analyzed and the main proposals proposed for reforming the present electoral system and their political consequences examined.

Israel's PR system has its roots in the institutions of the pre-state period. It had been introduced in the elections to the Zionist Congress and later in the elections to the Elected Assemblies of the Yishuv (the Jewish Community of Mandatory Palestine). The reason for its introduction in both cases was an effort to attract and maintain the support of the widest possible range of Jewish political groups so as to enable these institutions to exert authority without possessing sovereignty. Thus, the almost obvious recommendation of the Election Committee of the Provisional

State Council was that the Constituent Assembly, which later became the First Knesset, would be elected on the basis of a PR list system. In putting forth this system, the Committee was guided by three main considerations: (1) the PR system had deep roots in the tradition of pre-state institutions; (2) the decision applied only to the election for the Constituent Assembly; (3) the state of war (of the War of Independence) and general mobilization made it impossible to introduce a more complicated electoral system requiring the division of the country into constituencies.[1] Thus, what was originally ad hoc legislation became a permanent feature of the Israeli political system.

Nevertheless, adoption of the PR list system for election to the Knesset met with severe criticism from the very beginning. The most insistent advocate for replacing a nation-wide party-list PR system with a simple-majority system based on the British model was David Ben-Gurion.[2] He proposed that the country be divided into 120 constituencies, each of whose representatives would be elected by a simple majority. Ben-Gurion's proposal was, in fact, adopted by the party center of Mapai (the Labor Party) toward the end of the Second Knesset[3] and, starting with the Third Knesset, this plank was included in Mapai's platform in all subsequent election campaigns until the establishment of the Alignment in 1965.

Efforts to change the PR system intensified during the term of the Second Knesset (1951–5). The General Zionists put forward a proposal for raising the minimum electoral quota to 10 percent for the Third Knesset elections. This proposition formed part of the coalition agreement signed with Mapai on 26 December 1952.

Both Mapai and the General Zionists resumed their efforts to change the electoral system during the term of the Third Knesset (1955–9). In the debate on the type of electoral system that would be incorporated into the "Basic Law: The Knesset", Mapai proposed the simple-majority single-ballot system with 120 constituencies, whereas the General Zionists suggested a constituency-proportional system.[4] Both parties, however, failed to convince the Knesset to adopt either of their respective proposals. Contrary to the situation that had prevailed in the Second Knesset, when Mapai and the General Zionists together could produce an impressive majority of 65 Knesset members, their combined representation in the Third Knesset was reduced to 53 MKs. Thus, the opposition parties and the smaller coalition parties joined forces to defeat Mapai's proposal by 58 to 42; and the General Zionists' offering was rejected overwhelmingly by a vote of 58 to 11.[5] Having turned down these reform attempts, the Knesset went on to pass Section 4 of the "Basic Law: The Knesset", requiring an absolute majority in order to change the nation-wide PR list system.[6] A short time later, a coalition of the smaller parties succeeded in pushing through an amendment stipulating that Section 4 could be changed only if there were a majority (61 MKs) in all stages of the legislation process (i.e., in each of the three readings of the proposed bill).[7] Section 4 thus became one of the very few entrenched clauses in the whole of Israeli legislation.

The effort to reform the electoral system was renewed with the establishment of the Workers' Party (Rafi), formed by Ben-Gurion in 1965 after his departure from Mapai. The effort did not pick up any momentum, however, until the merger of Mapai, Rafi and Ahdut HaAvoda and the formation of the Labor Party in 1968. In July 1969, the Center of the Labor Party decided in principle to support changing the PR list system, and advocated a constituency-proportional system. The decision became a commitment by being incorporated into Labor's platform in the elections to the Seventh Knesset, held in October 1969.[8] Finally, during the third session of the Seventh Knesset, in 1972, the Labor Party tabled a private member's bill that proposed instituting a mixed constituency-proportional system. In this scheme 90 Knesset members would be elected from 18 five-member constituencies, and 30 members from a central list. In the preliminary vote, Labor's proposal was supported by the Free Center, the State List, and the Liberals (the former General Zionists) in the Likud.

For the first time in the history of the struggle for electoral reform, this bill was approved by the Knesset on preliminary consideration. Despite having received the required majority of 61 Knesset members, however, the bill did not proceed to its first reading, mainly because the liberals retreated from their support of the bill, claiming to be hamstrung by Herut warnings that any action by them to promote electoral reform would rock their joint Gahal bloc.[9] With the election of the Eighth Knesset in 1973, electoral reform was again pursued. The leader of the State List, Yigal Hurvitz, who had been a staunch supporter of Ben-Gurion, submitted a private member's bill that would institute a simple-majority, single-ballot system in the elections for the Ninth Knesset.[10] The proposal was rejected as being too radical, since it would involve changing an extreme proportional representation system into an extreme majoritarian system. Another proposal, on the other hand, calling for the introduction of a mixed proportional-constituency system, was referred by the Knesset to its Constitution, Law and Justice Committee for preparation for the first reading. According to this proposal, the majority of Knesset members would be elected in a number of multi-member constituencies and the rest on the basis of a country-wide list system.[11] Fierce objections arose from the National Religious Party (NRP), Mapam, and various other small parties; this resistance, coupled with the early termination of the Eighth Knesset's term, doomed the proposal, which never reached the plenum for the required first reading.[12]

The problem of electoral reform attained special importance during the election campaign to the Ninth Knesset in 1977. The demand for a change in the electoral law was stressed in the platforms of both the Alignment and the Likud. Herut – the major partner in the Likud – had continuously opposed a change in the electoral system because it feared that this would strengthen the Labor bloc; it now accepted the proposition of its partner, the Liberal Party, and agreed to support a moderate electoral reform. Electoral reform was almost the *raison d'être* of the Democratic Movement for Change (DMC), which had insisted that the single most important task of the Ninth Knesset should be the adoption of a new electoral law. Thereafter, in the DMC plan, the Ninth Knesset would dissolve and the elections for the Tenth Knesset would be held on the basis of the new system. Before its final decision to enter the cabinet, the DMC demanded that the country be divided into 20 four-member constituencies, with the remaining 40 members to be elected from a central list. The NRP, for its part, wanted no more than six constituencies electing a total of 80 members, the rest to be elected from a central list. The agreement that brought the DMC into the coalition fold stipulated that a proportional, multi-member district system should be adopted and put into effect for the elections to the Tenth Knesset.

A committee consisting of representatives of the coalition parties was established to work out the details. It was obliged to finish its work within nine months. The number of districts serving as the basis for the committee's deliberation ranged from six to sixteen.[13] Despite the repeated legislative initiatives of members during the term of the Ninth Knesset and despite the fact that more than three-quarters of its members represented parties committed to electoral reform, there was no concrete step forward in that direction from 1977 to 1981.

An attempt to introduce at least a partial change in Israel's electoral system was made during the first session of the Tenth Knesset (1981–4). A member's bill was introduced that would set a 2.5 percent threshold for all lists. The bill, however, was defeated by a relatively close vote (44 to 37). It is interesting to note that this bill, which was sponsored by a leader of the Likud and supported by some of the coalition partners in the Likud government, was opposed this time by Labor. The effect of the bill would have been to eliminate the small Arab lists, formed on a regional and personal basis, that traditionally supported Labor, as well as two tiny groups to which Labor was obligated for their cooperative voting.[14]

The issue of electoral reform seemed to have attained special urgency after the election of July 1984, when fifteen political parties gained representation in the Eleventh Knesset. That neither of the two major blocs, Labor and Likud, could form a viable coalition was attributed to the extremely divisive nature of the country's electoral system. The desire for reform, moreover, was reflected in the opinion polls. Whereas only 29 percent of the public favored a change to the system in 1965, 68 percent supported such a change in 1987.[15] In view of this impressive public support, 44 MKs decided to collaborate in tabling a members' bill to alter the present electoral system. They were successful in passing a preliminary motion to change to a mixed system in which 80 members would be elected in 20 four-member constituencies, and 40 from a central list. The proposed legislation was referred to the Constitution, Law and Justice Committee, which was charged to prepare a bill for the second reading.[16] It never reached this stage.

The most recent attempt at reform was made by a group of law professors from the Faculty of Law at Tel Aviv University who suggested a mixed electoral system as part of their proposed constitution for the State of Israel. Their proposal was based on the principles of the West German electoral system (they were examining these principles and adapting them to the Israeli situation before the reunification of Germany). Accordingly the country would be divided into 60 single-member constituencies, the representatives to be elected by a simple-majority vote. The remaining 60 Knesset members would be elected from a nation-wide list. There would be a 2.5 percent threshold, and successful parties would receive the number of seats proportional to their electoral strength, minus the number of seats they received in the constituencies.[17] If, for instance, a party received 50 percent of the total vote and won 40 seats in the constituencies, it would be entitled to 20 additional seats from the central list.

Although the Germans have had good experience with their electoral system, among scholars there has been a growing awareness of its shortcomings.[18] The Tel Aviv law professors' proposal to adopt it in Israel has met with serious criticism. Germany is a federation. It is a large country with a big population and with a deeply-rooted local and regional culture and tradition. The division of Israel into 60 single-member constituencies does not fit its distinctive centralistic tradition. It would create artificial entities without any roots in its culture or tradition and encourage undue fragmentation on the basis of local interests. Moreover, the MKs who would be elected from single-member constituencies by a simple majority would represent only a minority of their constituents. It is unthinkable that in a country like Israel with a highly politicized and ideologically fragmented political culture the voters would agree to be represented solely by a representative belonging either to the right-wing or the left-wing camp. Thus, while contests at the level of the single-member constituencies are conducive to two-party competition this does not fit multi-party systems. Finally, the professors' proposal ignores one of the main targets of an electoral reform in Israel, namely to provide the voter with an opportunity not only of choosing a party close to his or her political views, but also to vote for a favorite candidate. Single-member constituencies do not enable the voters to choose among candidates. In fact, single-member constituencies are no less list systems on a district basis, than the 120-member list system prevailing in Israel is on a nation-wide basis.

The Tel Aviv professors' proposed electoral reform passed the first reading by an impressive majority of 69 MKs and was referred to the Constitution, Law and Justice Committee shortly before the dissolution of the Eleventh Knesset, but it never reached the second reading.

Shortly after the elections to the Twelfth Knesset in November 1988, the attempts to reform the present electoral system were resumed. The Tel Aviv professors agreed to make a change in their proposal whereby 60 MKs would be elected in 20 three-member constituencies and the remaining 60 on a nation-wide list system.

The principles outlined in the revised proposal of the Tel Aviv professors served as a basis for deliberations of the Coalition Committee on Electoral and Government Reform established by the two main parties – the Alignment and the Likud – after the elections to the Twelfth Knesset. The proposed reform of the bi-partisan Committee was never adopted by the Knesset but it still serves as a blueprint for any possible reform of the electoral system to the Knesset. Therefore its principles and probable political consequences will be discussed on the basis of the results of the elections to the Twelfth (1988) to the Fifteenth Knessets.

3

Proposed Electoral Reforms for the Elections to the Knesset

The conviction that the social and political life of a nation can be improved by reforming the electoral system is not confined to Israelis. This view depends on the assumption that social and political process may be altered by means of constitutional changes in the electoral system. A clear instance of this line of thinking is Ferdinand Hermens' claim that the Nazis would not have come to power in Germany had a simple-majority electoral system been established under the Weimar Republic like the one in force in Britain.[1] Nor are the adherents of the simple-majority system alone in believing in the wonder-working potency of electoral laws. Van den Berg has proposed that had there been a system of proportional representation in Greece during the elections in 1920 then the entire course of the history of that country would have been different.[2] On the other hand, there have been others who have argued that in the period following the Second World War, the histories of the Scandinavian and Benelux nations, and of Switzerland, Austria and Germany, have shown that electoral systems and stability of government are the effect rather than the cause of social and political conditions.[3] In this regard Stein Rokkan has observed:

> Electoral systems have not changed in a vacuum. They function within culturally given contexts of legitimacy, and they are changed under the strains of critical "growing pains" in the development of the over-all constellations of national institutions.[4]

In a pioneer empirical study of the political consequences of electoral systems, Douglas Rae attempted systematically to overcome the principal impediment that stood in the way of earlier efforts in the field – namely the inability to predict the effects of changes in electoral laws. Thus he tells us:

If I were asked to predict the consequences of some alternative in an actual electoral law, it would be difficult or impossible to make a reliable deduction from this literature. One could repeat persuasive and insightful statements from the literature, but would certainly be unable to estimate the reliability of these statements. These are symptoms of a gap in our knowledge, and I have tried in this study to make a contribution toward it.[5]

In view of Lijphart's recent criticism of the flaws in Rae's analysis,[6] it seems important to test Rae's concepts, measurements and hypotheses, mainly regarding the effect of the district magnitude and the electoral formula, on the basis of the main proposals to reform the Israeli electoral system. Such an analysis will enable us to assess the validity of Rae's findings, and Lijphart's important modifications of Rae's method and findings, in the Israeli circumstances.

It might be argued that an analysis of the proposed reforms which was based on the results of the elections for the Seventh through the Fifteenth Knesset (1969–99), would not be reliable as regards radical changes in the voting patterns of the electorate that arose as a consequence of the full or partial adoption of such changes in the present electoral system. I am of the opinion, however, that although most of the proposals which have been put forward *would radically alter the Knesset election results*, they would not necessarily bring about a radical alteration in the way in which Israelis cast their ballots – at least in the short run.

Vernon Bogdanor[7] used a similar approach in comparing the results of the elections to the British House of Commons under the present simple-majority – single-ballot – "winner-takes-all" system with the hypothetical results under a proportional representation (PR) system, on the basis of simulations, or what he defines as "thought experiments". It is worthwhile to quote his justification for using this method:

> It might be objected that a thought experiment of the kind which we are intending to conduct is of little use . . . If Britain had a system of proportional representation, then, it can be argued, voting habits themselves would change . . . This objection is, in a sense, perfectly justified. But it is not very helpful, since it is quite impossible to predict precisely how voting patterns would change under an alternative electoral system. Let us, therefore make the simplifying assumption that the votes cast were exactly the same as in the 1983 general election but that the seats were allocated on a perfectly proportional basis.[8]

Another advantage of this approach, as we use it in our simulations, is that it enables us on the basis of the actual election results to the various Knessets to test *ceteris paribus*, not only the likely political consequences of the various proposals but also the validity of the assumed consequences of the various components of the electoral system, such as the district magnitude, the formula and the effective and legal thresholds.

I argue that any alteration of the electoral system at least in the short run is likely to effect only a modest change either in the behavior of voters or in the voting patterns. However, manipulating the formulae for allotting seats in the national legislature, and especially the district magnitude, by reducing the size of constituencies (i.e., changing the electoral system) or by increasing significantly the legal threshold, would make it possible to bring about a change in electoral results artificially. A consideration of the hypothetical consequences of the various proposals that have been put forward for changing the electoral system in Israel will elucidate the point.

I shall now proceed to examine the proposals for reforming the Israeli electoral system, and will concentrate on those that have been brought before the Knesset or mooted by the country's political parties, and which were a subject of debate when the issue was aired publicly.

1   A simple-majority electoral system on the British pattern, applied to 120 single-member constituencies. This plan was favored by David Ben-Gurion, and was tabled in the Eighth Knesset as a private member's bill by MK Yigal Hurvitz.

2   Raising the minimum electoral quota to 10 percent. This proposal was put forward by the General Zionists in the Second Knesset. And again, a much less radical proposal to raise the minimum electoral quota to 2.5 percent was proposed by the Likud in the Tenth Knesset, and adopted by the Constitution, Law and Justice Committee in the Fifteenth Knesset.

3   A division of the country into 30 three-member districts, with the remaining members of the Knesset elected from a nation-wide central list.

4   A proportional subdistrict system, in which the country would be divided into 14 constituencies equivalent to the current country's number of subdistricts. The allocation of Knesset seats would be made on the basis of the d'Hondt formula. This system was proposed by David Bar-Rav-Hai to his party, Mapai, which then submitted it for consideration by the Dov Yosef Committee.

5   A proposal similar to that of the proportional subdistrict system, with the difference that Knesset seats would be allocated according to the

Hare and Largest Remainder formula. This proposal was never officially put before the Knesset nor considered at any party forum. Its purpose was to determine the differences in the way that the d'Hondt and Hare formulae operate.

6   A division of the country into 18 five-member districts, with a nation-wide central list from which 30 remaining members of the Knesset would be elected. This plan was initially proposed by MK Gad Yaakobi as a private member's bill, and subsequently served as a basis for a preliminary bill in the form of a private member's bill that was tabled by a number of MKs from the Alignment at the beginning of the Seventh Knesset. The bill was accepted on a pre-committee hearing in the Knesset, as is the custom in the case of private members' bills, and laid down only two principles:

> (a) Some members of the Knesset would be elected in the constituencies, and others from a nation-wide central list.
> (b) An equal number of members would be elected from each constituency. A similar proposal was submitted by Yaakobi as a private member's bill in the Eleventh Knesset.

7   A division of the country into 24 five-member districts. Seats would be allocated on a nation-wide basis in accordance with the Hare formula; the allocation of the remaining seats would be carried out on the basis of the largest-remainder formula. Candidates would be elected by the "single transferable vote system" (STV). This proposal was tabled by Boaz Moab, with the backing of the Citizens' Rights Movement (CRM).

8   A proposal submitted by a group of Tel Aviv University law professors along the lines of the German electoral system. Accordingly the country would be divided into 60 single-member constituencies. The remaining 60 MKs would be elected on a nation-wide list system. The threshold would be increased to 2.5 percent.

The principles outlined in the revised proposal of the Tel Aviv professors served as a basis for deliberations of the Coalition Committee on Electoral and Government Reform established by the two main parties – the Alignment and the Likud – after the elections to the Twelfth Knesset in 1988.

The projections of the election results in the analysis which follows are calculated on the basis of the returns of the elections for the Seventh through Fifteenth Knessets.[9] The principal assumption here is that the adoption of most of the proposals above (proposals 1–8) would not only change the electoral system but substantially alter election results, in keeping with Rae's dictum: "electoral laws may create majorities where none are created by the voters".[10]

1 A Simple-Majority System

The most insistent advocate for replacing the nation-wide party-list PR system with a simple-majority system based on the British model was David Ben-Gurion.[11] Ben-Gurion's proposal was adopted by the party center of Mapai toward the end of the Second Knesset,[12] and starting with the Third Knesset it was included as a programmatic feature of Mapai's platform in all subsequent election campaigns.

According to this proposal, the country was to be divided into 120 constituencies, each of whose representatives would be elected by a simple majority. The major difficulty entailed in adopting the British system is that of determining how the country should be divided up into constituencies, and of preventing the gerrymandering of electoral districts. For the purpose of examining the consequences of instituting a simple-majority system in Israel, I have divided the country into 120 constituencies from north to south. In doing this I observed two conditions: (a) the preservation of geographical continuity in the case of each constituency; (b) adherence to the principle that constituencies should comprise more or less equal numbers of eligible voters. Electoral districting was determined on the basis of the map of the country's local councils and municipalities, and that of its regional councils.[13] The projection of the allotment of Knesset seats was derived first on the basis of returns in the Seventh Knesset elections. This was followed by a projection based on the election returns for the Eighth, Tenth and Eleventh Knessets. The number of voters that would have been contained in each constituency at the time of the Seventh Knesset elections was calculated on the basis of a national quota which was arrived at by dividing the overall number of eligible voters for the election by 120 Knesset seats, as follows:

$$\frac{1,748,710}{120} = 14,572 = \text{Quota per MK (Seventh Knesset)}$$

The effort to preserve the geographical integrity of the constituencies and to prevent gerrymandering resulted in a deviation in some electoral districts from the average number of eligible voters, which had been established for all of the constituencies. Thus the smallest constituency contained 8,436 eligible voters, and the largest 18,371 voters. The number of eligible voters in the remaining constituencies came close to the 14,572 mark that was established as our quota.[14] Therefore, on the basis of the proposed electoral districting and the returns in the elections for the Seventh Knesset, a simple-majority system of the British type, applied to 120 constituencies, would yield:

Alignment (Labor and Mapam)	103 seats
Herut–Liberal bloc	13
Agudat Yisrael	2
New Communist List	1
Minorities	1[15]

Our findings confirm a number of Rae's propositions concerning the consequences of a simple-majority system. However, they also invalidate one of the major propositions put forward by Rae. The following, then, are the propositions which are confirmed by the findings:

Differential Proposition One
The relative advantage of strong elective parties over weak ones found in all electoral systems tends to be greater under plurality or majority formulae than under proportional representation formulae.

Differential Proposition Two
Plurality and majority formulae tend to give a greater advantage to first parties than do proportional representation formulae.

Provisional Differential Proposition Three
Plurality formulae cause two-party systems (rejected).

Differential Proposition Five
Plurality and majority formulae tend to deny representation [in parliaments] to larger numbers of small parties than proportional representation formulae.[16]

And, finally, the proposition that under a simple-majority system,

strong parties with support evenly spread over many districts may win a preponderant majority of the seats [in parliament] with fewer than half the total votes.[17]

However, on the basis of our projection of the results of the simple-majority constituency system if applied to Israel, we would have to reject Rae's revised third proposition, namely:

Differential Proposition Three
Plurality formulae are always associated with two-party competition except where strong local minority parties exist, and other formulae are associated with two-party competition only where minority elective parties are very weak.[18]

Israel has no strong local political parties (as required by Rae's qualification of this proposition). Nevertheless the adoption of a simple-majority (on the basis of the election returns for the Seventh Knesset) formula in Israel would not only fail to produce a two-party system, but would actually create *a one-party system*.

In Britain the simple-majority constituency system usually has given rise to a two-party system because the difference in the electoral strengths of the country's two major parties, Labour and the Conservatives, was rather small – a circumstance that makes it possible for the government to change hands regularly. In every election held since the end of the Second World War until 1975, the differences in the number of votes obtained by the two parties have regularly fallen within the range of 0.5–6 percent of the total number of ballots cast.[19] Thus an average change of no more than 3 percent, and sometimes less, was enough to bring about a transfer of government from one party to the other. The second factor accounting for change in government consists in the more or less equal distribution of electoral support enjoyed by the two major parties among the constituencies. These two conditions, which had activated the pendulum of alternating rule between the leading political parties in Britain at least until the 1970s with relatively satisfactory regularity, *did not exist in Israel* in the period of the dominance of the Labor Party.

In the elections for the Seventh Knesset, the difference in electoral strengths between the two big Israeli parties came to as high as 25 percent, with the Alignment receiving 46.2 percent and Gahal 21.7 percent of the vote. During this election almost one out of every two voters had actually cast a ballot for the Alignment. Moreover, in Israel during the period of Labor dominance, 1949–77, the dominant Alignment had been alone among the country's political parties in enjoying electoral support, which was roughly equally distributed among electoral districts. The other parties obtained representation only in a few of those areas, in which they had large concentrations of their supporters.

A projection of returns for the Eighth Knesset elections under a simple-majority constituency system lends further support to the contention that had such a system been adopted in Israel during the Alignment's dominance, it would have established a one-party system. In that election a very significant change took place in the relative strengths of the two major party-blocs, that had the consequence of narrowing the margin of differences between them to about 10 percent: the Alignment (Labor and Mapam) won 39.6 percent and the Likud 30.2 percent of the total vote. Under a simple-majority constituency system, the reduction of the electoral gap between the country's largest party (Alignment) and the second largest (Likud) in the Eighth Knesset elections would have resulted in less dramatic changes than in the Seventh Knesset. However, the alignment would have still increased its lead considerably and returned a majority of two-thirds of the members of the Knesset.[20]

Projected Results in 120 Constituencies, Simple-Majority Single-Ballot System, Based on Actual Results of the Eighth Knesset – 1973

Alignment (Avoda–Mapam)	82 seats
Likud (Gahal–Laam)	34
Rakah	2
Arab lists	2

The data show, therefore, that under a simple-majority constituency system, during the period of dominance of the Labor Alignment, Labor would have obtained *in any possible alignment of parties* a majority of between two-thirds and five-sixths of the seats in the nation's legislature, thereby effectively establishing a *one-party system*. And although this situation would certainly ease the task of forming a stable government, the result would hardly be in keeping with the principles of a democratic system.

It is worthwhile in this regard to quote Duverger's observation that:

> The brutal application of the simple-majority, single-ballot system in a country in which multipartism has taken deep root would not produce the same results (i.e. a two party system), except after a very long delay. The electoral system works in the direction of bi-partisanism; it doesn't necessarily and absolutely lead to it in spite of all obstacles.[21]

However, when the gap in terms of voting support for the two major blocs narrowed significantly, as it did during the 1980s, as a result of the changing voting patterns of the electorate, even the introduction of the simple-majority formulae would have distorted the election outcomes only minimally. Thus, introducing the simple-majority system in the elections to the Tenth and Eleventh Knessets would have yielded the results detailed in table 3.1.

Table 3.1 Projected results in 120 constituencies, simple majority single ballot system, based on actual results of the Tenth and Eleventh Knessets

Party	Tenth Knesset – 1981			Eleventh Knesset – 1984		
	Percentage of vote	Projected results in seats	Actual results in seats	Percentage of vote	Projected results in seats	Actual results in seats
Likud	37.1	63	48	31.9	51	41
Alignment	36.6	53	47	34.9	66	44
Agudat Yisrael	3.7	2	4	1.7	1	4
Rakach	3	2	4	3.4	1	4
Shas	–	–		3.1	1	2
Total Projected		120			120	

The data presented in table 3.1 show that when the gap between the two largest parties narrows significantly, the introduction of a plurality system in the Israeli circumstances would result in a two-party system.

Table 3.2 The difference in the percentage of votes between the two largest parties in the elections to the Seventh, Eighth, Eleventh and Twelfth Knessets

Knesset / Party	Seventh 1969	Eighth 1973	Eleventh 1981	Twelfth 1984
Labor	42.2	39.6	36.6	34.9
Likud	21.7	30.2	37.1	31.9
Difference	24.5	9.4	0.5	3.0

Hence at least in Israel the extent of the gap between the two largest parties, rather than the presence or absence of strong local parties, would decide whether a one-party, or a two-party system would prevail under the plurality system.

2 A High Minimum Electoral Quota

In considering the impact of thresholds on the distribution of seats in the parliament it is necessary to distinguish between three types of thresholds:

1   Legal thresholds passed by the legislature.
2   Thresholds affected or defined by the size of the parliament (i.e., the number of members determined by law).
3   Most importantly – *effective thresholds*, defined by the laws of the electoral system.

The legal threshold is only one of the entry barriers that any group wishing to get representation in the Knesset has to overcome. Thus, for example, even without deciding on a legal threshold, no group attaining less than 0.83 percent – the percentage of valid votes required to get a seat in the Knesset (1/120) – would have attained representation in the Knesset.

Thus, deciding on the size of the parliament, in terms of determining the total number of its members, automatically set up a barrier of entry into the parliament. If, for instance, the Knesset were to decide that it should consist of only 60 members – the threshold would increase to 1.7 percent of the total valid votes.

In the First Knesset the d'Hondt formula was used in allocating the seats in the Knesset. No legal threshold was introduced. A legal threshold of 1 percent had been introduced in the elections to the Second Knesset in 1951, when instead of the d'Hondt formula the more proportional formula of Hare and Largest Remainder was introduced. The 1 percent threshold had been maintained until the elections to the Twelfth Knesset in 1988. Since 1992, until the present, the legal threshold has been slightly increased to 1.5 percent.

A proposal for raising the legal thresholds to 10 percent for the Third Knesset elections was first put forward by the General Zionists during the Second Knesset. This proposal formed part of the coalition agreement which was signed by Mapai and the General Zionists on 26 December 1952, and which contained a clause whose purpose was to deny Knesset representation to any party that failed to obtain at least 10 percent of the total vote in a parliamentary election. The Progressive Party, however, vigorously opposed the inclusion of the minimum-quota clause and, therefore, refused to join the coalition, until the offending clause was either shelved or annulled.[22] The reason for the Progressives' opposition to a high minimum electoral quota was simple arithmetic: it would have put an end to their party, which had never reached even 5 percent of the national vote in any election.

Mapai's support for a 10 percent quota stemmed from its wish to reduce the number of parties represented in the Knesset to between two and four major party blocs. Together, Mapai and the General Zionists were in a position to muster enough votes in the Knesset to obtain an absolute majority to ensure the passage of a minimum-quota bill.[23] In the end, however, Mapai was reluctant to press for the minimum quota prior to the Third Knesset elections, apparently out of consideration for the Progressive Party, which it regarded as a convenient coalition partner. The Mapai leaders preferred not to make the Progressives choose between having either to cease to exist or to merge with the General Zionists.[24]

For their part, the General Zionists were eager to absorb the Progressives and to consolidate administrative control within the party by brandishing the whip of this piece of legislation over the heads of the small factions in their ranks. With such a quota in force, any attempt by these factions to defy discipline by threatening to break away would be nipped in the bud. It was plain that these splinter groups would be unable to obtain the required minimum of votes in the next election if they chose to run on an independent ticket.

A projection of the hypothetical returns in the Seventh and Eighth Knesset elections under a 10 percent minimum-quota rule reveals that the consequence would have been to eliminate the small political parties, and to compel the merger of the country's religious parties. The result would have been the creation of a three-party system comprising Labor, the Likud and a Religious party bloc. It is difficult to believe that an imposed merger, brought about by a high minimum electoral quota, between the National Religious Party (NRP) and extreme religious parties such as Agudat Yisrael, would have led to the formation of more stable governments. The establishment of a three-party system would have had the effect of giving a pivotal role to the religious bloc, whose cooperation would have to be sought in order to establish a stable government.

The effort to introduce a higher electoral threshold – even though not as high as 10 percent, was renewed before the elections to the Tenth Knesset. MK Arens, on behalf of the Likud, proposed to the Labor Alignment to increase the 1 percent threshold to 2 percent, or 5 percent. The introduction of a 2 percent threshold would have decreased the number of parties in the Tenth Knesset from 10 to 7, and in the elections to the Eleventh Knesset from 15 to 9. Thus it probably would have a very moderate stabilizing effect.

The main purpose of those who call for an increase of the present legal threshold is to prevent the representation of small parties in the Knesset, thus reducing the number of parties and increasing the stability of the government. However, in view of the extreme division of the Israeli society and polity, though a minor increase of the legal threshold would eliminate a few small parties, it would not attain the major targets of its supporters, i.e., the stabilization of the government.

As a result of continuous pressure mainly by the large parties, and in spite of the strenuous opposition of the small and the religious parties, the threshold was finally slightly increased in March 1991 to 1.5 percent. This minor reform has only a small effect on the number of parties represented in the Knesset. It might encourage some small parties to merge, particularly in the Arab sector, but also in the religious camp and the extreme right. If the 1.5 percent threshold had been introduced in the elections to the Eleventh (1984) and Twelfth (1988) Knessets only two parties would have been barred from entering the Knesset, thus decreasing the number of parties in the Eleventh and Twelfth Knessets from 15 to 13 respectively. The parties that would have lost their representation in the Eleventh Knesset (1984) would have been Kach and Ometz, since each of them obtained only 1.2 percent of the votes, and the Progressive List of Peace (an Arab party) and the Arab Democratic List, each obtaining only 1.2 percent in the elections to the Twelfth Knesset (1988). Thus, in spite of the increase of the legal threshold in the elections of the Thirteenth Knesset (1992), 10 parties succeeded in getting representation in the Knesset, and in the election of the Fourteenth Knesset, 11 succeeded. In the election to the Fifteenth Knesset in 1999, 15 parties passed the legal 1.5 percent threshold. The extreme multiplicity of parties in the Fifteenth Knesset brought the Constitution, Law and Justice Committee in the Knesset to approve a proposed bill to increase the legal threshold again, from 1.5 percent to 2.5 percent (*Ha'aretz*, 6 June 2000). This bill was not submitted to the Knesset. However, due to the distinct polarization of the Israeli social and political system even an increase of the legal threshold to 2.5 percent would not significantly reduce the number of parties in the Knesset. Thus, if in the election to the Fifteenth Knesset the legal threshold had been increased to 2.5 percent only two parties ("One Nation" polling 1.9 percent of the vote and "Balad" getting 2 percent of the vote) would not have gained representation in the Fifteenth Knesset. The reduction of the number of parties from 15 to 13 is insignificant.

Only an increase of the legal threshold to 5 percent (as is the case in Germany, Russia and the Czech and Slovak Republics) would reduce significantly the number of parties in the Knesset. If such a threshold had been applied in the election of the Fifteenth Knesset it would have reduced the number of parties from 15 to 7. But such a drastic increase of the threshold has two shortcomings:

1   It would most probably compel relatively moderate parties to merge with more extreme parties of the same political camp. Thus the relatively moderate orthodox National Religious Party, which polled

4.2 percent of the vote, would probably enter into a political alliance with the ultra-orthodox "Jews of the Bible" party, which polled 3.8 percent of the vote in the elections to the Fifteenth Knesset. The new party would most probably take a more militant stance on religious issues, or might split after the election into two factions in the Knesset thus increasing again the number of parties. Splits of parties in the Knesset are quite a common phenomenon. Thus since the election of the Fifteenth Knesset two parties have split and the number of parties has reached a record of 17.

2   In order to prevent splits of parties after the elections it is imperative to pass a law which would allow mergers, but prohibit splits in legislative parties. However, it is questionable whether such a law has a chance to be enacted by the Knesset. Even if such a law were passed it would be impossible to prevent members of a Knesset party violating party discipline, unless such behavior involved serious sanctions against the "rebels" such as withholding some of their privileges as Knesset members.

The proposal to change the electoral system by increasing the legal threshold has been criticized for its manipulative and arbitrary nature. It would not bring about major changes desired by those who call for a reform of the present electoral system. It would not bring about a better representation of local interest or the establishment of a direct contact between the voters and their representatives. Nor would it lessen the influence of the party centers on the nomination of candidates to the Knesset. Moreover, the introduction of an arbitrary legal threshold that would bring about the elimination of some parties without attaining the above-mentioned benefits of a major reform in the electoral system would weaken the legitimacy of the democratic process.

In the light of the consequences that a high threshold would have for the political life in Israel, the view taken by Rae of the way in which the "mixed" electoral system works in the German Federal Republic does not appear to be entirely accurate – at least with regard to the effect it would have on the country's party system. According to Rae:

> The German plurality–proportionality formula appears to behave like a PR formula with respect to strong elective parties, but to impose a harsh plurality-like penalty upon weak elective parties.[25]

In Israel like in Germany it is not the plurality–proportionality formula which imposes a harsh penalty upon weak electoral parties, but rather the high 5 percent threshold.

The legal threshold is not the most effective barrier of entry to the parliament. The most effective barrier is the one inherent in the laws defining the electoral system. Thus, for instance, the introduction of the direct election of the prime minister on the basis of a majoritarian, two-ballot electoral system has set the effective threshold at 50 percent plus one vote. A candidate that is not capable of passing this very high threshold – in either the first or the second round – cannot be elected as prime minister.

The debate in Israel of the merits of increasing the present low legal threshold tends to ignore the fact that the most effective threshold would be attained by dividing the country into a number of constituencies. As a rule, the smaller the district the higher is the threshold and the more effective is the barrier of entry. Thus, dividing the present single-district constituency electing 120 members to the Knesset, into 40 three-member districts, or 30 four-member districts, or 24 five-member districts would automatically increase the effective threshold as defined by Lijphart and set it at 18.75 percent, 15 percent and 12.7 percent respectively.[26]

3 Proportional District Representation in 30 Three-Member Constituencies Combined with a Nation-wide Central List of Candidates

A bill containing a proposal for instituting a proportional district electoral system in which the country would be divided into 30 three-member constituencies, with the rest of the members of the Knesset being elected from a nation-wide central list of candidates, was mooted first by the General Zionists, who tabled it in the form of a private member's bill in the Third Knesset.[27] A similar plan was also passed as a majority proposal in the Dov Yosef Committee, which was formed with the establishment of the Israel Labor Party at the beginning of 1968, for the purpose of reviewing the electoral systems in use abroad as well as in Israel. Its findings and recommendations were to be submitted to the Labor Party center so that they might be incorporated in the party's campaign platform during elections for the Seventh Knesset.[28] The committee's proposal differed from that of the General Zionists on the question of the formulae of apportionment of seats as regards both the constituencies and the central list of candidates.

However, before undertaking to discuss the differences between the two proposals, I would first like to consider the principal features of the plan which was worked out by the General Zionists, and then to project the returns that would have been obtained under this system were it in force in the Seventh Knesset elections.

District-Proportional Elections

For the purpose of the said "District-Proportional Elections" bill, these shall signify the following:

1 The country shall be divided into thirty electoral districts;
2 the number of voters in each electoral district shall be equal insofar as possible;
3 each electoral district shall be geographically continuous;
4 only three members of the Knesset shall be elected in each district;
5 elections in each district shall be proportional, subject to the conditions set out below;
6 a candidate list in an election shall appear as a candidate only in a single electoral district;
7 a person eligible for election shall appear as a candidate only in a single electoral district;
8 in the apportionment of seats for each electoral district, only those lists shall be counted in a given district which have received at least 20 percent of the ballots that were cast, and the quota required for the election of each representative shall be at least 20 percent of the number of ballots cast in said district;
9 a list which appears in at least three electoral districts shall be eligible to submit a nation-wide list;
10 a candidate who appears on a district list may appear as a candidate on the nation-wide list;
11 thirty or more seats shall be apportioned among the nation-wide lists;
12 if no representatives are elected in one or more electoral districts – in consequence of the limitation in paragraph 8, above – then all of the said seats shall be added to the apportionment among the nation-wide lists;
13 in the apportionment of seats among nation-wide lists, only those nation-wide lists shall take part of which at least four representatives were elected from their district lists in four electoral districts;
14 for the purpose of apportionment of seats among nation-wide lists, all surplus votes shall be taken into account of the district lists which are associated with each of the nation-wide lists that are eligible to take part in the apportionment, in accordance with what is laid down in subparagraph 13, above;

15 no transferal of surplus votes shall be allowed between district lists in electoral districts, nor shall transferal of surplus votes be allowed between nation-wide lists;

16 a member of the Knesset whose seat has been vacated in consequence of his decease, resignation, or for any other reason –

(a) If the said member of the Knesset whose seat has been vacated was elected on a district list, his seat shall be taken by a candidate who was on the list which included said member's name, and whose own name immediately follows the name of the last of the elected candidate.

(b) If the said member of the Knesset whose seat has been vacated was elected on a district list, and there are no more candidates on that list, then a by-election shall be held in that same district, in accordance with the rules laid down above.

(c) If the said member of the Knesset whose seat has been vacated was elected on a nation-wide list, his seat shall be taken by a candidate who was on the list which included said member's name, and whose own name immediately follows the name of the last of the elected candidates.[29]

The proposal of the General Zionists differs from that of the Dov Yosef Committee principally in two respects. In the General Zionists' proposal, the quota for each representative in each of the electoral districts is set as 20 percent of the votes cast in the district. And should there be no representatives elected in a given district because none of the candidates had accumulated a sufficient number of votes to meet the quota of 20 percent of the district votes, then all of these seats will be added to those which are to be apportioned among the nation-wide central lists. Thus according to the proposal of the General Zionists, *at least* 30 Knesset members will be elected from the central list, and the apportionment of seats nationally will be carried out only among those party lists which returned *at least* four members in four electoral districts. On the other hand, according to the proposal of the Dov Yosef Committee, the allotment of seats in the case both of electoral districts and of the central lists would be calculated on the basis of the same formulae as were used until the elections for the Eighth Knesset (i.e., the Hare and largest-remainder formulae), and only 30 members would be elected from the nation-wide central list.

For the purposes of comparing the consequences that might be expected if the two systems were put into practice, the country was divided into 30 three-member constituencies containing, insofar as possible, nearly equal numbers of eligible voters, and which were geographically continuous and self-contained (just as was done when we considered the case of an electoral districting based on 120 constituencies). The following (table 3.3), then, are the results of a projection of the hypothetical election returns for the Seventh Knesset under the system proposed by the General Zionists.

The big parties enjoy an obvious advantage in the electoral districts. However, because of the high quota specified per Knesset member (20 percent of the total number of votes in a district), there would be only two members elected in 15 of the electoral districts – so that a total of 15 seats would be added to the central list. And since only the Alignment and Gahal would have returned four members in four constituencies, the surplus votes would have had to be apportioned solely between these two parties. Moreover, because the Alignment would have retained a large number of members from the electoral districts, the number of its surplus votes would be reduced to nearly the number of Gahal's surplus votes. Thus Gahal would have obtained almost half of the total of seats contested on the central list, as opposed to a quarter of those in the constituencies.

The system proposed by the General Zionists would have increased the strength of Labor by about 40 percent and of the Likud by as much as 58 percent, as compared with their actual strengths in the Seventh Knesset. And although this proposal would have enhanced the power of the opposition, it would have given the party in power almost a two-thirds majority of seats in the Knesset.

The preceding analysis of returns in the Seventh Knesset elections under the system proposed by the General Zionists confirms Rae's findings that small constituencies with few members subvert the principle of proportionality: "small district magnitudes tend to concentrate seats in the already strong parties".[30] Let us now consider what the results would have been if the majority proposal of the Dov Yosef Committee had been put into effect in the Seventh Knesset elections, as compared with the actual apportionment of seats for that Knesset term. The Dov Yosef system differs from the one which was in force prior to the changes introduced for

Table 3.3   The distribution of seats on the basis of the General Zionists Proposal (based on the Seventh Knesset [1969] election results)

	Emet*	Gahal**	Total
Number of MKs elected from Districts	56	19	75
Number of MKs elected from the Central List	23	22	45
Total	79	41	120

* Emet – The Israeli Labor Party, later to become the Alignment.
** Gahal – The Likud party list.

the Eighth Knesset in respect of the apportionment of electoral districts, but not as regards the allotment of Knesset seats. The Dov Yosef proposal provided for a division of the country into what amounted to 31 constituencies: these comprised 30 three-member electoral districts plus one nation-wide district of 30 members. Under the existing system, on the other hand, the country is treated as consisting of a single electoral district.

Until the passage of the Bader–Ofer amendment, the system for allotting Knesset seats relied on the Hare and the largest-remainder formula. As compared with the results under the system used in the Seventh Knesset, the projected returns that would have been obtained had the Dov Yosef proposal been put into effect at the time would therefore have been as set out in table 3.4.

Thus, according to the Dov Yosef proposal, the main beneficiaries would have been the two major parties the Labor Alignment and Gahal. They would have increased their representation in the Knesset significantly – the Labor Alignment by 25 percent and Gahal by 27 percent. The losers would have been the small and medium-sized parties, which would have lost from 75 percent to 25 percent of their representation in the Seventh Knesset.

The comparison thus confirms Rae's assertion that in the case of small constituencies (in the case of the Dov Yosef Committee proposal the district magnitude would have been $M = 3$), even an extreme proportionality formula would not result in a proportional apportionment of seats:

Table 3.4 The distribution of seats according to the Dov Yosef proposal

	AMT	B	HL	G	Min	LA	AM	W	D	Total
In Districts	56	5	26	2	1	–	–	–	–	90
Nationwide	14	3	7	1	1	1	1	1	1	30
Total	70	8	33	3	2	1	1	1	1	120
Actually in the Seventh Knesset	56	12	26	4	4	4	4	3	2	

AMT – The Labor Alignment
B – The Mafdal
HL Gahal
G – Agudat Israel
Min – Minorities
La – Independent Liberals
AM – State List
W – Democratic List for Peace – Rakah and the Black Panthers
D – Agudat Yisrael Workers

"Very small [district] magnitudes, of say, three seats, will thwart even the most precise PR formulae in its practical effect."[31]

Our findings support as well Rae's claim concerning the importance of the effect of district size on election returns:

> I would suggest that too much attention is generally given to the effects of electoral formulae, while too little is given to the effect of district magnitudes. The data reported here show quite clearly that the proportionality of electoral formulae depends heavily upon the number of seats assigned to each district.[32]

The findings of the Dov Yosef Committee are even more radical on this point. Applying four different formulae to election returns in the Sixth Knesset election, under a system of 30 three-member constituencies and a central list of 30 candidates, the Committee arrived at the findings as set out in table 3.5.

It is evident from both the findings of the Dov Yosef Committee and our own results that the country's largest party (i.e., the Alignment) is at an advantage in small electoral districts even when an extreme proportionality formula is applied.[33]

4 Proportional Subdistrict Representation

A proposal by which the country would be divided into 14 constituencies based on the administrative division of Israel into subdistricts was submitted by David Bar-Rav-Hai a number of times for consideration, first by Mapai and then by Alignment–Labor.[34] Bar-Rav-Hai's plan offers a

Table 3.5   Findings of the Dov Yosef committee

	30 three-member districts 30 members on central list	
Largest-remainder formula: Alignment without Mapam (Hare & largest remainder)	73	–
Largest-remainder formula: Alignment with Mapam	78	(70)[a]
d'Hondt formula: Alignment without Mapam	84	–
d'Hondt formula: Alignment with Mapam	83	–

Source: Gad Yaakobi and Ehud Gera, Ha-hofesh livhor ("Freedom to Choose") (Tel Aviv: Am Oved, 1975), p. 65.

[a] Represents projections based on election returns for the Seventh Knesset.

number of advantages. First, it requires no redrawing of electoral districts and thereby also eliminates the possibility of gerrymandering. Second, it ensures that every ballot would have very nearly equal weight, regardless of where in the country the voter who had cast it resided. Finally, the particular virtue of the proposal is that it corrects the most serious flaws in the present electoral system while leaving the country's multi-party structure and proportional representation intact. We can obtain an idea of how Bar-Rav-Hai's proposal would work by projecting the returns under that system for the Seventh and Eighth Knesset elections, respectively.

On the basis of the Seventh Knesset election returns, therefore, 120 Knesset seats would be apportioned in the following manner:

Alignment (Labor Party and Mapam)	74 seats
Gahal (Herut and Liberal bloc)	29
Mafdal	8
Arab parties	3
Rakach and Agudat Yisrael, each	2
Independent Liberals and State List, each	1

According to Bar-Rav-Hai's proposal the apportionment of seats is determined by the d'Hondt formula, which requires that seats be distributed among rival political parties on the basis of the average "payment" in ballots by a party for each seat in parliament, as follows:[35]

$$\text{``Average''} = \frac{\text{Total Ballots}}{\text{Total Seats} + 1}$$

It is Rae's contention that "unless district magnitudes are very great, the highest average formula will handicap small parties".[36] And, indeed, the projection of returns in the Seventh Knesset elections under the system proposed by Bar-Rav-Hai confirms both Rae's assumption and our own prediction that his plan, like those which preceded it, *would not only change the electoral system but would also substantially alter election results*. Had a proportional subdistrict system been administered, in combination with the d'Hondt formula, in the elections for the Seventh Knesset, it would have drastically changed the relative parliamentary strengths of the country's political parties, and would have given Labor an absolute majority of 74 seats in the Knesset.

Were the d'Hondt formula applied to the 14 subdistricts enumerated in the table, during elections for the Seventh Knesset, the Alignment would have increased its electoral strength by 32 percent and Gahal by 12 percent, as compared with their actual showing at the time. Similar though less extreme results would have been obtained had Bar-Rav-Hai's proposal been put into effect during the Eighth Knesset elections.

Since electoral support for the Alignment (51 seats as against 56 in the Seventh Knesset) fell and that of the Likud (39 seats as against 26 in the Seventh Knesset) rose significantly, with the consequence that the electoral gap between them was drastically reduced, the projected results under the d'Hondt formula would have given the Alignment a less substantial advantage than in the elections for the Seventh Knesset. Even so, applying the d'Hondt formula to 14 subdistricts would yield, in the case of the Eighth Knesset elections, an increase of 18 percent (from 51 to 60 seats) in the strength of the Alignment and 8 percent (from 39 to 42 seats) in that of the Likud.

The particular difficulty in the way of apportioning Israeli constituencies along the lines of the country's division into administrative subdistricts is the great size of the Tel Aviv subdistrict. On the basis of the country's current 14 subdistricts, Tel Aviv alone would have been represented by fully 41 Knesset members. That many representatives would make it impossible to hold personal elections in the Tel Aviv constituency, whose contests would have to be run on the basis of a proportional party-list system. Bar-Rav-Hai therefore specifies that the subdistrict of Tel Aviv should be redrawn to accommodate a number of geographically contiguous constituencies in such a way as to give the ballot of every voter as nearly equal weight as possible.

Following Bar-Rav-Hai's recommendation, therefore, the two small two-member subdistricts of Kinneret and Safed would be merged to form a single four-member constituency; and the subdistrict of Tel Aviv would be broken up into three constituencies: North Tel Aviv, with 11 members;[37] Central Tel Aviv, with 19 members;[38] and South Tel Aviv, with 11 members.[39] On this basis, the country would be divided into 15 constituencies, the number of whose representatives would range from 3 members in the Ramla subdistrict to 19 members in the subdistrict of Tel Aviv. This would be a reasonable apportionment of constituencies in point of district magnitude.

In many of the countries that have adopted a proportional district system (e.g., Finland, Norway, Sweden, Switzerland, Belgium) the number of parliamentary representatives ranges between 2 and 35 members.[40] As regards the average magnitude of constituencies, moreover, the proposal to divide the country into 15 electoral districts is well in line with the practice in most countries in which the proportional district system is in force. Such an apportionment of constituencies in Israel would yield an average district magnitude of 8 representatives. In Sweden the average magnitude of an electoral district is 8.2, and in Switzerland, 8 representatives. There are a number of countries in which the average district magnitude is greater: 13.3 in Finland, 19.1 in Italy, and 13 in Luxembourg.[41]

An analysis of the consequence of dividing the country into 15 electoral districts confirms Rae's claim that increasing district magnitudes[42] (in our case by turning the subdistrict of Tel Aviv into three constituencies, each with a smaller number of representatives) works to the advantage of the big parties, although only moderately.[43] Applying the d'Hondt formula to Seventh Knesset returns, had the country then been divided into 15 constituencies, reveals that the parliamentary representation of the large parties would have increased, and that concomitantly the number of the country's Jewish political parties would have been reduced from 13 to 6. The effect of adopting this program would be the creation of a three-party system. Thus the Alignment would have received 76 seats; the Herut–Liberal bloc 29; the National Religious Party 9; Agudat Yisrael 1; Rakach 2; and the Arab lists 3.

Had the same system been applied in the Eighth Knesset elections, the results would have been similar – although, as already observed, the electoral advantage accruing to the Alignment would have been less extreme.

Thus the Alignment would have received 61 seats; the Herut–Liberal bloc 43; the National Religious Party 7; the Independent Liberals and Rakach, each 3; Arab lists 2; and Agudat Yisrael 1.

5 Proportional Representation in Subdistricts: The Hare Formula versus the d'Hondt Formula

In this section a comparison will be made between results obtained with the Hare and d'Hondt formulae in constituencies of equal magnitude. Rae argues that different formulae for apportioning seats under a proportional representation system yield similar results. The differences are significant only if the magnitudes of electoral districts are changed. In this regard he asserts:

> For some purposes I will need to call upon the distinction between these (PR) formulae, but this should not becloud the major perspective: PR formulae are generally similar to each other in practical effect.[44]

Thus, if the d'Hondt formula had been used instead of the Hare and the

Largest Remainder (LR) formula in the elections to the Seventh Knesset (1969) in the 14 subdistrict constituencies, the number of parties would have decreased from 13 to 8.

Moreover, as compared with the Hare formula, that of d'Hondt would increase the electoral strength of the country's largest party (Alignment) by 28 percent (from 58 to 74 seats). At the same time it would seriously undermine the parliamentary representation of medium-sized parties, and eliminate entirely ephemeral parties (i.e., those that had obtained fewer than three seats in the Seventh Knesset). These findings run counter to Rae's assertion that

> the difference between PR formulae are blurred when district magnitude is allowed to vary. Indeed the mechanics of the formulae depend largely upon district magnitude. Any of these formulae will behave more like a different formula applied at the same level of district magnitude, than like the same formula at a very different level of magnitude.[45]

On the basis of our findings we can say that with regard at least to districts of medium magnitude (M = 8.63), the d'Hondt formula produces results that differ from those obtained by means of the Hare formula. Under the d'Hondt formula the dominant party would gain an obvious advantage whereas medium-sized and small parties would be put at a distinct disadvantage electorally.

Similar results are obtained in the results of applying the d'Hondt and Hare formulae had the country been divided into 14 electoral districts at the time of the Eighth Knesset elections.

Thus in the case of the Eighth Knesset, as well, the d'Hondt formula would increase the electoral strength of the Alignment by 22 percent (from 49 by applying the Hare formula to 60 seats by applying the d'Hondt formula) and that of the Likud by 5 percent (from 40 to 42 seats respectively), and decrease that of the Mafdal from 14 seats under the Hare formula to 8 under d'Hondt. It would also significantly reduce the strength of medium-sized and small parties, and effectively create a two-and-a-half-party system.

The most striking difference in the results of applying the d'Hondt in comparison with the Hare and the Largest Remainder formula in districts of medium magnitude (M = 8.6) occurred when the medium-sized third largest National Religious Party, which until the election to the Ninth Knesset held 8–10 percent of the vote, was reduced to a bare 3 percent in the elections to the Eleventh Knesset in 1984.

Thus while applying the Hare and Largest Remainder formula to our 14-subdistrict division, on the basis of the actual results of the elections to the Eleventh Knesset (1984), it would have, as in the case of the Eighth Knesset (1973), slightly reduced the strength of the large party (Alignment) by one seat, from 44 to 43 seats, and slightly reduced the number of parties from 15 to 12. The application of the d'Hondt formula would actually create a two-party system – the Alignment gaining 62, the Likud 56, and Rakach, with its electorate heavily concentrated in the Lower Galili – 2.

Our examination of four of the preceding proposals for changing the electoral system in Israel (the plurality system, the introduction of a high threshold, PR district representation in 30 three-member constituencies and a 30-member national district, and PR subdistrict representation using the d'Hondt formula) confirms our main hypothesis *that these electoral reforms would significantly alter the results of elections to the Knesset to the advantage of the parties that put these proposals forward.* The only proposal that would have only a minor effect on election results, but would substantially alter the electoral system, is that of proportional subdistrict representation in which parliamentary seats would be apportioned on the basis of the Hare and the Largest Remainder (LR) formula. The great advantage offered by the LR formula is that it would correct a number of the faults of the current system – without at the same time undermining the multi-party structure of the political life of the country, and without requiring an arbitrary apportionment of constituencies. A division of the country into 14 electoral districts would not only allow for more effective representation of local interests, but would establish closer ties between the electorate and Knesset members, and would in some measure loosen the control of party centers over the selection of candidates.The system would also contribute to the stability of governments, insofar as it would enhance the electoral strength of the big political parties and weaken that of smaller ad hoc political formations. Moreover, the fact that under this system the representatives of the country's urban areas would be significantly in the majority offers the advantage of putting a restraint on the forces of local patriotism and regional particularism.

The major disadvantage of the subdistrict approach is, as noted, the magnitude of the Tel Aviv–Jaffa subdistrict. Applying the Hare and LR formula to a proportional representative system with 15 constituencies, on the basis of the actual results to the Seventh Knesset (1969), would also have a moderate effect on election results by eliminating small parties (those with up to two members in the Seventh Knesset), and would have reduced the number of parties from 13 to 7. Thus the Alignment would have received 59 seats, the Likud 29, the NRP 14, the State List 5, Agudat

Yisrael 4, Independent Liberals 3, Rakach 3 and the Arab lists 3.

Results similar to these are obtained with regard to the returns in elections for the Eighth Knesset. Apportionment of the ballot under the Hare and Largest Remainder formula in the Eighth Knesset elections would have had the effect of slightly reducing the strengths of the two large parties (Alignment and Likud) by canceling the advantage they obtained from the Bader–Ofer amendment. Applying the Hare formula to elections in constituencies based on the division of the country into subdistricts would increase the electoral strength of Israel's medium-sized party (NRP), which would increase its representation in consequence of surplus votes in a number of districts. The number of parties would have been reduced from 10 to 8.

The same conclusion applies to the results of the elections to the Eleventh Knesset in 1984. The appliance of the Hare and LR formula would be almost identical with the actual results and the number of parties would have been slightly reduced (from 15 to 12).

6 Proportional District Representation in 18 Five-Member Constituencies in Conjunction with a Nation-Wide Central List (Yaakobi Proposal)

MK Gad Yaakobi has proposed that the current PR system be changed to one based on the principle of proportional representation by constituency. Accordingly, he proposes that 30 members of the Knesset be elected in a general election under a proportional system on the pattern of the one which is currently in force, and that the 90 remaining members be elected in 18 five-member constituencies.[46]

Projected results of the Yaakobi proposal

I shall begin by considering the effects of the Yaakobi proposal had it been adopted in the Seventh Knesset elections, and follow with an analysis of election results for the Eighth Knesset as calculated on the basis of three different formulae: (1) that of Yaakobi: (2) the d'Hondt formula: (3) the Hare and LR formula.

Nationwide
Section 8 of Yaakobi's private member's bill requires that a minimum

Table 3.6   The probable results of the Yaacobi Proposal at the national level based on the Seventh Knesset (1969) results

Party	No. of seats allotted nationwide (Total 30)	Percentage Total seats nationwide (Total 30)	Percentage from total seats nationwide (Total 120 in the Seventh Knesset)
Alignment	16	53.3	46.6
Gahal	7	23.3	21.7
NRP	3	10.0	10.5
Agudat Yisrael	1	3.3	3.3
Independent Liberals	1	3.3	3.3
State List	1	3.3	3.3
Minorities	1	3.3	3.3

quota be set in the allotment of Knesset seats. Any party obtaining less than 3 percent of the total of valid ballots that have been cast will not take part in the apportionment of the 30 seats contested in the nation-wide election. In the case of the Seventh Knesset elections, this rule would have eliminated five parties – Poalei Agudat Yisrael, the Free Center, the Israel Communist Party, New Communist List, and Ha-Olam Ha-Ze–Koah-Hadash.

On the basis of the nation-wide electoral quota[47] and the Yaakobi formula, the apportionment of the 30 seats contested in the general election is as set out in table 3.6.

Examining the Yaakobi proposal on the basis of the returns of the Seventh Knesset elections, we find that in regard to the nation-wide contest for 30 of the 120 Knesset seats a significant advantage would have been obtained by the strongest party, and a slight advantage by the second strongest party. However, each of the country's medium-sized parties (namely Agudat Yisrael, Independent Liberals, State Lists and Minorities) would have merely held on to its electoral strength, and the small parties would have obtained no representation. Thus the Alignment would have increased its strength nation-wide by about 7 percent, and Gahal by 1.6 percent. The remaining parties that were able to meet Yaakobi's minimum electoral quota would have received the same percentage of parliamentary seats as they actually obtained in the Seventh Knesset.

By district

The Yaakobi plan specifies that the average magnitude of 18 districts, each being a five-member constituency, should be calculated by the following formula:

Quota determining district size = eligible votes: 18.

On the basis of the total number of eligible voters, the average magnitude of an electoral district in the elections for the Seventh Knesset would have been 97,150. The formula for calculating the quota per Knesset member for each district would be:

District quota = Total valid ballots: 5.

Thus the district quota would be 20 percent of the total valid ballots. According to the Yaakobi proposal, the electoral quota for each representative would be two-thirds of the district quota, in other words, about 13 percent of the total of valid ballots per district.

A mere glance at the returns of the Seventh Knesset elections shows that only the Alignment and Gahal received more than 13 percent of the nationwide total of votes. Hence the proposed minimum electoral quota for the constituencies would have given the bulk of parliamentary seats to the two big parties and to a number of smaller parties whose supporters were concentrated in large numbers in certain areas of the country.[48] Thus if the quota for determining district magnitudes that was proposed by Yaakobi were applied in 18 districts which were geographically contiguous and which contained as nearly equal numbers as possible of eligible voters the result, on the basis of the Seventh Knesset elections, would be: Alignment 59, Gahal 27, NRP 2, Arab lists 2.

On the basis of these figures, and adding the seats gained by each party in the nation-wide contest, the projected apportionment of seats under the Yaakobi proposal in the Seventh Knesset would be:

Alignment	75
Gahal	34
NRP	5
Agudat Yisrael	1
State List	1
Independent Liberals	1
Arab lists	3

Yaakobi's proposal would therefore have given an absolute majority of seats to the Alignment and increased the strength of Gahal. It would have also greatly reduced the representation of medium-sized political parties and taken the country's small parties out of the running. The results would have been much the same had the proposal been put into effect in the Eighth Knesset elections.

7 Apportionment of the Country into 24 Five-Member Districts (Moab Proposal on Behalf of the Citizens' Rights Movement)

The system and its advantages
According to the proposal of MK Boaz Moab,[49] Knesset seats would be apportioned on the basis of the PR system that was in force in the country until the Eighth Knesset elections – that is to say, on the basis of the Hare and LR formula. The number of seats allotted to each party would be determined by the nation-wide electoral quota; and surplus votes that were not used up in the constituencies would be placed in a general pool from which they would be apportioned among candidates on the nation-wide central party lists, in accordance with the size of their remainders.

The major change contained in the Moab proposal concerns the election of candidates. Moab proposes that the country be divided into 24 electoral districts of roughly equal size. Each would be a five-member constituency. Not only would the voter have the opportunity of voting for the party of his choice, but he could also rank the candidates on the party list in the order of his preference on the basis of the principle of the "single transferable vote" (STV).

The advantage of the procedure recommended by Moab is that it corrects a number of shortcomings in the present system, without the results of elections being affected by the manner of the apportionment of electoral districts. The proposal would therefore prevent the gerrymandering of constituencies.

Three principal advantages would derive from dividing the country into 24 electoral districts. Regional interests would be better represented in the nation's parliament; a stronger connection would be established between voters and their representatives; and the control over the selection of candidates by party centers would be significantly weakened. Putting the Moab proposal into effect would therefore result in greater consideration being given to the political views and aspirations of the public at large.

It is unlikely that such a system would weaken the government by undermining party discipline. Elected representatives would continue to be dependent on the financial and organizational backing of their local party branch. Moreover, a member of the Knesset would find it difficult to withdraw from his or her party and set up as an independent candidate, as it is possible to do under the current system. On the other hand, parliamentary party factions would exert greater influence on decisions than is the case at present, because governments would be compelled to seek to persuade Knesset members of their own factions to support their policies since the latter would no longer be dependent on the favor of the central party leadership.

However there are a number of disadvantages to the Moab proposal that have to be taken into account:

1   Moab's principal innovation is his inclusion in his proposal of the STV procedure. But the way in which the procedure is applied in this particular proposal distorts the very principle of the system that Moab clearly wishes to establish. The special benefit deriving from the adoption of STV is that it allows for personal voting within the framework of the PR system. However, in the Moab proposal, STV has the function only of allowing the voter to rank candidates on the list of the particular party he or she is supporting in the election. In this instance the principle of the "preferential vote" would have served better – in other words, a system that would allow the voter to indicate the candidate most favored on the list of the party of choice. The use of STV in an electoral system based on party lists would needlessly complicate the business both of voting and of counting ballots. Under a personal ballot system, the principle of the STV electoral system allows the voter to support candidates of his choice on lists other than that of the party of choice, whereas according to the Moab plan the voter has only the option of voting for candidates appearing on a single party list. In Israeli conditions, even the country's biggest party could not return more than three of its five candidates in any district. Voters should therefore be allowed to indicate no more than two or three of their preferences among candidates. But they should be *required*, as well, to select one of these two or three candidates as the most favored choice, just as under the STV system the voter is obliged to indicate preference for at least one candidate.

2   The Moab proposal weakens the control of the central authority only of the major parties, and not of the country's small parties. The great majority of candidates put forward by the big parties would be elected in the constituencies, whereas most small-party candidates would be elected on the basis of surplus votes transferred to the central pool, and would therefore consist of the candidates appearing on the nation-

wide party lists. These lists are put together for the most part by the central institutions of parties rather than the local branches in the constituencies.

3 Notwithstanding the claims that the proposed system is constituency oriented, the requirement of an electoral quota nationally in fact guarantees that even the smallest parties would obtain Knesset representation on a nation-wide basis.

8 The Proposal of the Bi-Partisan Coalition Committee on Electoral and Government Reform

Soon after the elections for the Twelfth Knesset in November 1988, the attempts to reform the present electoral system were resumed. The Tel Aviv professors now altered their proposal: 60 MKs would be elected in 20 three-member constituencies and the other 60 on a nation-wide list system. This revised proposal served as a basis for the deliberations of the Coalition Committee on Electoral and Government Reform convened by the two main parties – the Labor Alignment and the Likud – after the elections for the Twelfth Knesset. That Bi-Partisan Committee came to the conclusion after several months of deliberation that there must be a change in Israel's electoral system according to the following principles:

1 The electoral system should be proportional on a national basis and personal on a constituency basis. Sixty members of Knesset would be elected in 20 electoral districts, three from each district, and 60 members of Knesset would be elected from a national list.

2 Full proportionality would be maintained in the representation of parties in the Knesset. The distribution of seats would be determined by the results of the election on the national lists.

3 The number of members of the Knesset would be fixed at 120, as far as possible. Expert opinion and proposals would be solicited for a technical method of preserving full proportionality while maintaining the size of the Knesset at 120. These proposals should be studied and discussed in the Constitution, Law and Justice Committee of the Knesset in its deliberations on reforms in the electoral system.

4 The threshold would be fixed at a minimum of four members of Knesset.

5 The method of voting would be as follows:
(i) Each eligible voter will have two ballots. One ballot is for the voter's choice of party in the national list.

(ii) The second ballot will list all candidates for election in the voter's district. The voter will mark his/her two preferred candidates (two are required) whether they are of the same party or of two different parties.

6 Each list of the constituency ballot will include the names of three candidates. (The general list of candidates up for election will be constituted of all the party lists.)

7 The three candidates who receive the most votes in each district will be elected, on the condition that they belong to parties or lists which pass the national threshold. If an electee is disqualified, he/she will be replaced by that candidate from the same party who has received the next greatest number of votes. If there are no candidates from the same party remaining in the constituency, then the next candidate in line on the national list of the same party will assume office.

8 The boundaries of the electoral districts will be drawn by a committee of three who will be appointed by the president of the Supreme Court.
(i) A candidate will be allowed both to be included on a national list and to run in an electoral district. Knesset membership will be supplemented by those elected from the national list on the basis of national proportionality.
(ii) The members of the committee will bring the resolutions made in this proposal for approval to the authorized bodies of their respective parties.
(iii) The above principles will be included in a proposed Basic Law of the Knesset, which is currently under deliberation and which is on the agenda of the Constitution, Law and Justice Committee. If amendments and modifications of this proposal are proposed during the course of the deliberations, they will be brought before the Coalition Committee for Electoral and Government Reform.

The reform proposed by the Bi-Partisan Committee is, not surprisingly, in favor of the two largest parties – the Likud and the Labor Alignment, but the reform also has serious shortcomings which perhaps were inevitable if an agreement was to be reached that was acceptable to both parties. One of the shortcomings is the fact that the proposed threshold will be fixed at a minimum of four members of the Knesset, meaning that a party which wins up to three Knesset seats in the districts but none in the national list, will be denied representation in the Knesset. This violates the very principle of district representation which the division of the country into constituencies aimed to achieve. Moreover, it amounts to unseating a representative who had been duly elected by his constituency.

Another shortcoming of the proposed reform is that the voter is entitled to two ballots – one for his preferred party and one for the candidate of his choice. Although this grants the voter a significant influence in electing his preferred two candidates, it tends to increase party fragmentation in the parliament as has been the case in both France and West Germany with their system of two-ballot voting.[50] This is exactly the opposite of one of the major aims of the proposed reform: to have a more limited number of parties in the Knesset.

These shortcomings of the proposal by the Bi-Partisan Committee could be rectified in one of the following ways. First, by eliminating the two-ballot system; each voter would be entitled to vote only for a party list, but would be entitled to indicate preference among the candidates on the list. This method is used in Finland and its adoption in Israel would enable the voter to indicate a within-party preference while preventing the negative impact of the panachage (cross-party voting, used for instance in Switzerland) in party fragmentation in parliament. Second, it is possible to determine the threshold in percentages and not in absolute numbers. The Bi-Partisan Committee's proposal to set a four-MK threshold would then be the equivalent of a 3.3 percent threshold. A party would be entitled to participate in the allocation of seats if it attained either 3.3 percent of the total votes or elected at least one candidate in a constituency. This would prevent the unseating of a duly elected district candidate but, on the other hand, it would tend to increase party fragmentation and would therefore be less desirable than the first alternative. A third possibility would be to entitle a party to get representation in the Knesset even if it does not attain the required 3.3 percent threshold, but elects at least one representative in the district, by increasing the total number of MKs. This means that, as is the case in Germany, the total number of MKs would not be fixed. (In Germany, when a party wins more directly-elected seats than it has been allocated, in a particular region, that party will none the less retain all the regional seats it has won and the size of the *Bundestag* would simply increase, as has occasionally happened.) The disadvantage of this method in the Israeli circumstances stems from the fact that the apparently minor change of even one extra seat could have a major impact on the fortunes of one of the main parties. For example, after the 1988 elections, the leader of the Likud was asked to form a government because the Likud had won just one seat more than the Labor Alignment: 40 against 39. Finally, it must be pointed out that although the Bi-Partisan Committee recommended that full proportionality must be maintained in the representation of parties in the Knesset, the details of its proposals for electoral reform show that the principle of proportionality might be distorted at both the district and the national levels.

Table 3.7 Projected distribution of seats in fourteen constituencies electing sixty members and a sixty-member National List by the d'Hondt, Hare and LR formulas based on the Twelfth (1988) Knesset Election returns and a 3 percent threshold

Sub-District Constituencies[a]	Total sub-District	Alignment[c]		Ratz		Likud		Mafdal		Agudat Israel		Shas		Rakach[c]	
		D[b]	H	D	H	D	H	D	H	D	H	D	H	D	H
Jerusalem	5	2	1			3	2			0	1	0	1		
Safed & Kinneret	2	1	1			1	1								
Afula & Nazareth	4	2	1			1	1			0	1			1	1
Akko	4	2	1			1	1	0	1					1	1
Haifa	6	3	2	0	1	3	2			0	1				
Hadera	3	2	1			1	1							0	1
Hasharon	3	2	1			1	1							0	1
Petah-Tikva	5	2	2			3	2	0	1						
Ramla–Rehovot	5	2	2			3	2			0	1				
Tel Aviv	6	3	2	0	1	3	2					0	1		
Ramat Gan	5	3	2			2	2			0	1				
Holon	5	2	2			3	2					0	1		
Ashkelon	3	1	1			2	1					0	1		
Beersheba	4	2	1			2	2					0	1		

Sub-District Constituencies[a]	Total sub-District	Alignment[c]		Ratz		Likud		Mafdal		Agudat Israel		Shas		Rakach[c]	
		D[b]	H	D	H	D	H	D	H	D	H	D	H	D	H
District Total	60	29	20	0	2	29	22	0	2	0	5	0	5	2	4
Compensation on National Basis	60	15	24	6	4	16	23	6	4	7	2	7	2	3	1
Grand Total	120	44	44	6	6	45	45	6	6	7	7	7	7	5	5
Actual Twelfth Knesset	104[d]	39	39	5	5	40	40	5	5	5	5	6	6	4	4

[a] We have been unable to divide the country into twenty 3-member constituencies, as proposed by the bi-partisan committee, because the committee does not stipulate how the boundaries of the electoral districts are to be drawn. So we have based our projection on the present division of the country into 14 administrative sub-districts, each allocated a number of representatives according to the number of eligible voters residing in the district. However, an attempt by a geographer to divide the country into twenty 3-member constituencies using the d'Hondt formula yielded exactly the same results that we arrived at in the 14 sub-districts, cf. Stanley Waterman, Hadashot (Hebrew daily), 21 May 1989, p. 5.

[b] D = d'Hondt formula, H = Hare formula and LR.

[c] See Glossary.

[d] Eight parties which won sixteen seats in the Twelfth Knesset would not be granted any representation.

The d'Hondt formula currently in use in Israel favors the large parties; Victor d'Hondt wished to encourage small parties to merge in order to reduce the number of such parties and to help to provide more stability for the party entrusted with the government of the country. The d'Hondt formula allocates seats according to the highest average of votes each party obtains in an election. The Hare formula, which was in use in Israel from 1951 to 1969, favors the small parties; but if the 60 seats at the district level were allocated according to the d'Hondt formula, then almost all of them would be given to the two largest parties.

A projected distribution of seats in 14 constituencies electing 60 members and a 60-member national list by the d'Hondt and by the Hare and LR formulae, based on the Twelfth Knesset election returns and a 3 per cent threshold, would have given the following results at the district level: the d'Hondt formula would have allocated the 60 seats by giving 29 to the Labor Alignment and 29 to the Likud with the remaining two to Rakach; but the Hare formula would have given only 20 to the Alignment, 22 to the Likud, while the small parties would have also gained seats: two to Ratz, two to Mafdal, five to Agudat Israel, five to Shas, and the remaining four to Rakach. In this projected distribution, the 120 seats would be distributed among seven parties, because eight parties which won 16 seats in the Twelfth Knesset elections would not be granted any representation. See table 3.7, which demonstrates also the relative strength of the parties in the 14 district constituencies.

Moreover, the principle of full proportionality would be even more significantly distorted at the national level. The Committee's proposal states: "The distribution of the seats will be determined by the results of the elections for the national lists." This means that the total number of additional seats allocated to each party would be determined by a quota arrived at by dividing the total number of votes by the total number of the 60 national-list seats, not by dividing them by the total number of the district and national seats, namely 120. Only the second quota guarantees full proportionality to all parties attaining the required threshold. The first quota would cut the representation of the small parties virtually by half, since almost none of them would gain any seats at the district level. See table 3.8, which clearly shows the difference in the impact of applying the two methods at the national level.

If the Bi-Partisan Committee's proposed reform had been adopted in the elections to the Twelfth Knesset in 1988, several political consequences would have followed:

Table 3.8 Projected distribution of seats in fourteen constituencies electing sixty members and a sixty-member National List by the d'Hondt formula based on the Twelfth Knesset Election returns and a 3 percent threshold

Sub-Districts Constituencies	Total sub-District	Alignment	Ratz	Likud	Mafdal	Agudat Israel	Shas	Rakach
Jerusalem	5	2		3		0	0	
Safed & Kinneret	2	1		1				
Afula & Nazareth	4	2		1		0		1
Akko	4	2		1	0			1
Haifa	6	3	0	3		0		
Hadera	3	2		1				0
Hasharon	3	2		1				0
Petah-Tikva	5	2		3				
Ramla–Rehovot	5	2		3	0	0		
Tel Aviv	6	3	0	3			0	
Ramat Gan	5	3		2		0		
Holon	5	2		3			0	
Ashkelon	3	1		2			0	
Beersheba	4	2		2			0	
District Total	60	29	0	29	0	0	0	2
Compensation on National Basis	60	22	3	23	3	3	3	3
Grand Total	120	51	3	52	3	3	3	5
Actual Twelfth Knesset	104	39	5	40	5	5	6	4

1   *threshold*: by increasing the threshold from 1 to 3 percent, there would
    have been only seven parties not 15;
2   *formula*: using the d'Hondt formula, the calculation of the total
    number of additional seats on the basis of the 60 national-list seats
    (instead of on the basis of the total number of 120 seats) would signif-
    icantly decrease the representation of the small parties and thus greatly
    benefit the two largest parties at both the district and the national
    levels;
3   *district magnitude*: the district magnitude would be small (M = 3) and
    there would probably be disproportionate results at the district level.

However, if the additional 60 seats at the national level are used to
compensate parties in order to achieve full proportionality, then a
projected distribution of seats in 14 constituencies electing 60 members and
a 60-member national list by the d'Hondt formula, based on the Twelfth
Knesset election returns and a 2.5 percent threshold, would yield proportional results and would allow nine parties instead of seven to obtain
representation. See table 3.9, which shows the difference in calculating the
60 seats at the national level on the basis of full compensation to all parties
in order to achieve full proportionality.

Since the Bi-Partisan Committee's proposed reform still serves as a blueprint for any possible reform of the electoral system, I have tested its
possible consequences also on the basis of the results of the elections to the
Thirteenth (1992), Fourteenth (1996) and Fifteenth (1999) Knessets.

According to my simulations (see tables 3.10, 3.11, 3.12, in which the
distribution of seats by parties in the 14 district constituencies is shown) the
number of parties under the present 1.5 percent threshold, using either the
Hare or the d'Hondt formula, would remain the same: 10, 11, and 15
respectively in the Thirteenth, Fourteenth and Fifteenth Knessets.

Even an increase of the threshold to 2.5 percent as proposed by the
Constitution, Law and Justice Committee in the Fifteenth Knesset
(*Ha'aretz*, 6 June 2000) would have only a minor impact on the number of
parties represented in Knesset. It would have reduced the number of parties
in the Thirteenth Knesset from 10 to 7; in the Fourteenth Knesset from 11
to 10; and in the Fifteenth Knesset from 15 to 13.

Using the Hare and LR formula in the proposed mixed 14 districts, and
one nation-based constituency, in the election to the Thirteenth Knesset
would have increased moderately the representation of the third largest
party, Meretz (from 12 to 15 seats), and the representation of Shas in the
Fourteenth Knesset (from 10 to 13 seats). It would make only a slight
difference in the representation of the three largest parties (Israel One,

Table 3.9 Projected distribution of seats in fourteen constituencies electing sixty members and a sixty-member National List by the d'Hondt formula based on the Twelfth Knesset Election returns and a 2.5 percent threshold

Sub-Districts Constituencies	Likud	Tehiya	Alignment	Ratz	Mapam	Rakah	Shas	Mafdal	Aguda Israel	Total
Jerusalem	3		2							5
Safed & Kinneret	1		1							2
Afula & Nazareth	1		2			1				4
Akko	1		2			1				4
Haifa	3		3							6
Hadera	1		2							3
Hasharon	1		2							3
Petah-Tikva	3		2							5
Ramla–Rehovot	3		2							5
Tel Aviv	3		3							6
Ramat Gan	2		3							5
Holon	3		2							5
Ashkelon	2		1							3
Beersheba	2		2							4
District Total	29		29			2				60
Compensation on National Basis	14	4	12	6	3	3	7	5	6	60
Grand Total	43	4	41	6	3	5	7	5	6	120
Actual Twelfth Knesset	40	3	39	5	3	4	6	5	5	110*

* The SixParties which won ten seats in the Twelfth Knesset would not be granted any representation.

Table 3.10 Projected distribution of seats in fifteen constituencies electing sixty members and a sixty-member National List by the d'Hondt formula based on the Thirteenth Knesset Election returns and a 1.5 percent threshold

Sub-District Constituencies	Alignment		Meretz		Likud		Tzomet		Moledet		Mafdal		United Torah Judaism		Shas		Hadas		Arab Democratic Party	
	D	H	D	H	D	H	D	H	D	H	D	H	D	H	D	H	D	H	D	H
Jerusalem	2	1		1	2	1							1	1		1				
Safed & Kinneret	1	1			1	1														
Afula & Nazreth	2	1			1	1												1		
Akko	2	1		1	1	1											1	1		
Haifa	4	3		1	2	1		1												
Hadera	1	1			1	1														
Hasharon	2	1		1	1	1														
Petah-Tikva	3	2		1	2	1		1												
Ramla–Rehovot	3	2		1	3	2		1												
Tel Aviv	4	3	1	1	2	2		1												
Ramat Gan	3	2		1	1	1		1				1	1							
Holon	3	2			1	1														
Ashkelon	1	1			2	1										1				
Beersheba	2	1		1	2	1										1				
Judea and Samaria					1	1														
District Total	33	22	1	9	23	17	0	5	0	0	0	1	2	1	0	3	1	2	0	0
National Total	23	21	6	6	16	15	4	4	1	1	3	3	2	2	3	3	1	3	1	2
Total Number of seats	56	43	7	15	39	32	4	9	1	1	3	4	4	3	3	6	2	5	1	2
Actual 13th Knesset	44		12		32		8		3		6		4		6		3		2	

Table 3.11 Projected distribution of seats in fifteen constituencies electing sixty members and a sixty-member National List by the d'Hondt, Hare and LR formulas based on the Fourteenth Knesset Election returns and a 1.5 percent threshold

Sub-District Constituencies	Alignment		Meretz		Likud		Maidal		United Torah Judaism		Shas		Moledet		Hadash		Third Way		Yisrael Ba'aliya		Arab Democratic Party	
	D	H	D	H	D	H	D	H	D	H	D	H	D	H	D	H	D	H	D	H	D	H
Jerusalem	1	1			2	1	1	1	1	1		1										
Safed & Kinneret	1	1			1	1																
Yizrael	1	1			1	1										1			1			
Akko	1	1		1	1	1										1			1		1	1
Haifa	3	2			3	2			0	0						1				1		
Hadera	1	1			1	1														1		
Hasharon	2	1			1	1		1				1										
Petah-Tikva	3	2			2	1		1				1										
Ramla-Rehovot	3	2	1	1	3	2		1				1										
Tel Aviv	3	2			2	2						1							1	1		
Ramat Gan	2	1			1	1			1	1		1										
Holon	2	1			2	2																
Ashkelon	1	1			2	1					1	1	0	0	0	0	0	0				
Beersheba	1	1			2	1					1	1			0	0						
Judea and Samaria					1	1																
District Total	25	18	1	2	25	19	1	4	2	2	2	8	0	0	0	3	0	0	3	3	1	1
National Total	18	16	5	5	16	15	5	5	2	2	4	5	1	1	3	3	2	2	3	4	1	2
Total Number of seats	43	34	6	7	41	34	6	9	4	4	6	13	1	1	3	6	2	2	6	7	2	3
Actual 14th Knesset	34		9		32		9		4		10		2		5		4		7		4	

Table 3.12 Projected distribution of seats in fourteen constituencies electing sixty members and a sixty-member National List by the d'Hondt, Hare and LR formulas based on the Fifteenth Knesset Election returns and a 1.5 percent threshold

Sub-District Constituencies	Alignment		Mafdal		United Torah Judaism		Democratic Arab		Hadas		Moledet National Bloc		Shinui		Yisrael ba'aliya		Israel Our Home		One Nation		Likud		Meretz		United Arab List		Center		Shas	
	D	H	D	H	D	H	D	H	D	H	D	H	D	H	D	H	D	H	D	H	D	H	D	H	D	H	D	H	D	H
Jerusalem	1	1			1	1						1									2	1							2	1
Safed & Kinneret	1	1				1																							1	1
Yizrael	1								1	1												1								
Akko	1	1					1	1	1	1											1				1	1				
Haifa	3	2											1	1	1	1					1	1							1	1
Hadera	1	1																			1	1			1	1				
Hasharon	1																				1	1								
Petah-Tikva	2	1		1																	1	1					1	1	1	1
Ramla–Rehovot	2	1											1								1	1	1	1		1			2	1
Tel Aviv	2	2																			1	1	1	1					1	1
Ramat Gan	2	1																			1	1	1	1					1	1
Holon	2	1			1	1															1	1	1	1					1	1
Ashkelon	1	1													1	1					1	1					0	0	2	1
Beersheba	1	1													1	1					1	1					0	0	2	1
District Total	21	16	0	2	2	3	1	2	2	2	0	1	0	2	3	3	0	0	0	0	13	11	2	5	3	2	2	0	15	10
National Total	14	12	3	3	3	3	1	1	1	2	2	2	3	3	3	3	1	2	2	1	10	9	5	5	2	2	3	3	9	8
Number of seats	35	28	5	5	4	5	2	3	3	4	2	3	3	5	6	6	1	2	2	1	23	20	7	10	5	4	3	5	24	18
Actual 15th Knesset	26		5		5		2		3		4		6		6		4		2		19		10		5		6		17	

Likud and Shas) in the Fifteenth Knesset, each gaining either one or two additional seats. Thus, it would have increased the representation of Israel One from 26 to 28 seats, the Likud from 19 to 20 seats, and Shas from 17 to 18 seats.

The introduction of the d'Hondt formula would have made a difference in the Thirteenth Knesset, when the gap between the largest party (Labor) and the second largest party (Likud) amounted to 27.2 percent (44 seats and 32 respectively). This might have helped the late Prime Minister Rabin to establish a more stable coalition consisting of two parties – Labor and Meretz.

When the system became an extreme multi-party system, with the two major parties together polling between 55 percent in the Fourteenth Knesset and 37.5 percent of the votes in the Fifteenth Knesset, using the d'Hondt formula instead of the Hare formula would have made no substantial difference as to the ability of coalition formation by the two major blocs: the center–left Labor bloc, and the center–right Likud bloc.

The mixed electoral system proposed by the Bi-Partisan Committee would hardly create a more stable and effective government in the extremely polarized Israeli multi-party system. Yet, using the d'Hondt formula would have some salutary influence. It would have increased the representation of the three major parties in the Thirteenth Knesset (1992). The representation of the Labor Party would have increased by 42 percent, and that of the Likud by 22 percent. In the elections to the Fourteenth Knesset (1996) it would have increased the representation of the Labor Party by 26 percent, and that of the Likud by 28 percent. In the elections to the Fifteenth Knesset, when the extreme fractionalization of the Knesset created an extreme multi-party system, with three parties getting an almost equal share of seats, it would have increased the representation of Israel One by 35 percent, Likud by 17 percent, and Shas by 41 percent. Finally, the division of the country into fourteen constituencies would make for a more balanced representation by introducing a territorial element into the existing system, emphasizing only sectorial representation. It would also make for a closer contact between the MK and his or her constituency, and thus make the political system more responsive and accountable.

Conclusions

Our projections of the results of adopting three of the major proposals considered above in the case of the Seventh and Eighth Knesset elections (i.e., the simple-majority system applied in 120 electoral districts, the subdistrict system applied in 14 districts under the d'Hondt formula, and the proposal to divide the country into 18 five-member districts and a nation-wide constituency from which the remaining 30 MKs would be elected), confirm Rae's general proposition, which states:

> The effect of electoral laws upon the competitive positions of political parties in legislatures is marginal by comparison to the effect of election outcomes.[51]

This rule explains why, as a result of the Alignment's decline in electoral strength by about 7 percent and the Likud's increase in strength by about 9 percent in the Eighth as compared with the Seventh Knesset elections, the Alignment would have lost a substantial number of parliamentary seats both under the simple-majority system and under the Yaakobi proposal in conjunction with the d'Hondt formula. In the first instance the Alignment's representation would have fallen from a hypothetical 103 seats in the Seventh Knesset to 82 seats in the Eighth Knesset; and in the second, its representation would have dropped from a hypothetical 74 to 62 seats in the Seventh and Eighth Knessets, respectively.

However, notwithstanding the Alignment's absolute decline in number of seats in the Eighth Knesset because of its poorer showing in the elections, each of the three proposals would have significantly augmented that party's relative strength both in the Seventh and Eighth Knessets as a result of the "manufactured" changes they would have introduced into the electoral process.

The results of the comparison tend to support Rae's insistence that under a PR constituency system:

> Most single-party parliamentary majorities are "manufactured" by electoral system.[52]

The absolute majority that the Alignment would have obtained under the system being considered here would have actually been the effect of changing the electoral system. Thus the Alignment would have enhanced its strength by about 60 percent in the Eighth Knesset if a plurality constituency system was in effect in 120 electoral districts; and the same party would have enjoyed a gain in strength of about 20 percent if a PR constituency in force in 14 or 18 districts and a nation-wide constituency was used under the d'Hondt formula. This situation would be similar to that of Norway where that country's Labor Party obtained an absolute parliamentary majority after receiving less than 40 percent of the total vote, under a PR constituency system with the Saint Lague formula, whose effect is similar to that of the d'Hondt formula.[53]

In urging the advantages offered by their proposals the advocates of electoral reform in Israel have ignored the fact that changes in the electoral system have significant political consequences with regard to the relative representation of parties in the Knesset.

1   Our analysis of the consequences for electoral reform, which have been widely publicized and publicly discussed in Israel – the simple-majority system, the proposal for a 10 percent minimum electoral quota, the two slightly differing plans proposed by the General Zionists and the Dov Yosef Committee to divide the country into 30 three-member electoral districts and a central list from which the remaining Knesset members would be elected, and the proposals of Gad Yaakobi and Bar-Rav-Hai for a proportional subdistrict system – confirm our principal thesis *that all of these proposals would not only change the electoral system but would also substantially alter the results of elections.*

2   Our findings confirm most of the general propositions of Rae and are therefore useful in helping us to predict the broad effects of proposed changes in the country's electoral system.

3   However, two of Rae's more specific propositions are not supported by the findings:
   (a) The claim that a district-plurality system will *inevitably* produce a two-party system, except in countries with strong local parties. Israel, however, has no strong parties organized on a local basis; nevertheless, if a district-plurality formula was adopted in Israel, it would in some instances result in a one-party rather than a two-party system.
   (b) Our findings do not confirm the proposition that, under a PR system applied to relatively large constituencies with the same number of representatives, different formulae would produce similar results. In Israel, the d'Hondt formula would produce significantly different results from those that derived from the Hare and LR formula – in both the case of a division of the country into 14 subdistricts and the modified plan of dividing the country into 15 electoral districts, as well as under the proposal of establishing 18 five-member districts in combination with a nation-wide constituency in which 30 members of the Knesset would be elected.

4   The Moab proposal, according to which the country would be divided into 24 five-member districts, with parliamentary seats apportioned nationally on the basis of the Hare and LR formula, would not change

the results of parliamentary elections. The proposal does, however, favor the interests of the country's small parties, so that it is unlikely to be supported by Israel's major political parties.

5   The reform advocated by the Bi-Partisan Committee would achieve some of the targets of the various proponents of electoral reform in Israel. The division of the country into 20 constituencies could enable local interests to be given special attention. The election of representatives on a constituency basis would enhance the accountability and responsiveness of the MKs and would decentralize the nomination process. The introduction of preferential voting at the district level could increase the influence of the voters' choice of candidates. However, the critics of that proposed reform stress that it would weaken the parties, reduce party cohesion in the Knesset, and put undue emphasis on local issues in a country which still faces the challenge of a number of major national problems. They add that there might still be the necessity of forming coalition governments, in which the religious parties still would, in all probability, play a pivotal role.

Finally, one should bear in mind what Stein Rokkan noted about electoral systems: they function "within culturally given contexts of legitimacy, and they are changed under the strains of critical 'growing pains' in the development of the over-all constellations of national institutions". In Israel, it is in the interest of the small parties and of the religious parties, as well as of the party machines and bureaucracies of the large parties, to preserve the existing PR system with all its defects. These parties therefore resist any change. However, in my considered opinion, the fact that none of the proposed electoral reforms is likely to remedy all the deficiencies of a political system should not deter Members of the Knesset from using electoral engineering to achieve at least some of the desired targets.[54] They would be well advised to follow the exhortation of the Salvation Army: "Save the world, one soul at a time".[55]

4

The New Premier–Parliamentary System in Israel

We are generally correct in our criticism of the polity under which we live but often wrong in assessing the alternatives and their hoped for benefits.[1]

The relationship between the executive and the legislature is one of the most important institutional differences between democracies.[2] Based on these relations, there are six major institutional arrangements prevailing in western democracies: the presidential system; the semi-presidential system of the Fifth French Republic; the *régime d'assemblée*, which existed under the Third and Fourth French Republics; and as Sartori points out, three types of parliamentary systems that are characterized by the authority structure in which the prime minister, as the chief of the executive branch, is called upon to perform his duties as (1) a first above unequals (as in Britain), (2) a first among unequals (as in Germany), and (3) a first among equals (as in Israel until 1996).[3]

The Main Characteristics of the Former Parliamentary System

From the establishment of the State of Israel in 1948 until the elections to the Fourteenth Knesset in 1996, Israel maintained a parliamentary system of government. A parliamentary system is defined as one that requires governments to be appointed, supported, and, as the case may be, dismissed by parliamentary vote.[4]

Within the framework of the parliamentary system, the prime minister of Israel was regarded as *primus inter pares* (first among equals), even though he or she actually enjoyed a special status. The prime minister presided over cabinet meetings and set out the cabinet's agenda, was the chief spokesman of the government and instructed the cabinet members in important foreign and domestic policy issues. Prime ministers initiated important decisions, such as the Camp David Accords (Menachem Begin) and the Oslo Accords (Yitzhak Rabin). Within the constraints of the coalition system, the prime minister appointed and presented his cabinet to the Knesset. If the prime minister resigned, so did his cabinet. Since 1981, the prime minister has had the power to dismiss ministers.

Contrary to the common notion that the Israeli parliamentary system was weak and unstable, it is my contention that it held some impressive features of a stable, strong system. The average duration of a cabinet, since the establishment of the state until the introduction of the premier–parliamentary system in 1996, was close to 2.5 years.[5] The average duration of the parliament elected for a term of four years was 3.6 years. Moreover, in terms of effectiveness and subject to the agreed upon coalition program, the powers of the Israeli government in both foreign and domestic matters were impressive. In the realm of foreign affairs, the cabinet had the power to declare war without the consent of the Knesset and to conduct war without proper consultation with its Foreign and Defense Relations Committee. The cabinet could also carry out its foreign and defense policy without any serious impediments being posed by the opposition. In the realm of domestic affairs, the government was the prime initiator of both financial and regular legislation. The Knesset had only limited control over the budget and no power to change it. The government had the power to issue by-laws, and thousands of regulations were issued without proper and effective control by the Knesset. Emergency regulations could alter any law, suspend its effect or modify it, and also impose or increase taxes or other obligatory payments.

As long as the government enjoyed a majority in the Knesset, the Knesset had very limited control and influence on the government. There was continuous public complaint about insufficient participation of its members in plenary sessions and the activities of the committees. The latter had no real powers, such as being able to subpoena witnesses or to compel government members to appear before them. Party discipline was strong, and the voters' influence on their representatives was nil.

Reasons for Changing the Parliamentary System

The parliamentary system's main deficiencies stemmed from the fact that it occasionally became difficult to establish viable coalition governments.

This had a serious impact on the stability and effective functioning of the political system.

It has been necessary to establish coalitions because Israel has a polarized and fragmented party system. The number of parties contesting for seats, from the election to the First Knesset in 1949, until today, has varied between 14 and 31, and the number of parties gaining representation has varied between 10 and 15. The multi-party system reflects the five basic cleavages dividing Israeli society, namely, those between religious and secular sectors, Sephardic and Ashkenazi Jews, Jews and Arabs, rich and poor, and doves and hawks. The heterogeneous nature of Israeli society is reflected also in the way Israel has elected its parliament, the Knesset. Since the establishment of the state, Israel has adopted an extremely proportional country-wide list system.

However, from the elections to the First Knesset in 1949, to 1977, the Labor Party's dominance and its pivotal position enabled it to establish stable coalitions. Only in the 1980s did the coalition system's deficiencies come to the fore. The party system became extremely polarized. It was divided into two major blocs: the Likud, which is right of center, and Labor, which is left of center. The two blocs were distinctly divided by three major overlapping cleavages. The Likud bloc's electoral support was mainly based on the Sephardic, religious and hawkishly oriented voters, while the Labor bloc's electoral support came mostly from the Ashkenazi, secular and dovishly oriented voters. Neither bloc was able to form a stable coalition, and therefore, in 1984, they agreed to establish a National Unity government.

The first National Unity government (1984–8) functioned quite effectively, due to the need to deal with two major crises: the war in Lebanon, which had to be resolved quickly, and the containment of rampant inflation. After attaining both these goals, cooperation deteriorated between the two major parties.

The 1988 elections again failed to produce a clear verdict, hence the two major parties reluctantly formed a second National government. Since this second National Unity government was not based on an agreed platform, immobility became its hallmark. Neither partner could agree on a common program to further the peace process, and the government disintegrated.

The crisis that finally toppled the government was initiated by Labor against the Likud's intransigent position toward the peace process. In March 1990, the Labor Party managed to assemble a bare majority of 61 out of the 120 Knesset members, and, together with other parties, won a no-confidence vote that brought down the second Unity government. This was the first time in the history of the Israeli parliamentary system that a government was forced out of office by a no-confidence vote. Labor was unable to form an alternative government, however, due to the defection of some of its supporters in the no-confidence vote. Consequently, a crisis ensued which lasted for almost three months, during which both Labor and Likud tried to outbid each other in order to attain the support of the religious parties and some individual Knesset members in order to form a narrow government. Finally, the Likud succeeded in forming a narrow coalition. Thus the notorious "filthy trick" of Labor failed and brought about a major public outcry for the reform of the political system.[6] As Diamond and Sprinzak point out:

> In fact, the three-month crisis was unprecedented in only one sense: It starkly exposed the malfunctioning of the Israeli system of government and, more than ever before, made most Israelis aware of the problem. But almost everything that took place between March and June of 1990 had happened before: coalition horse trading; political blackmail and extortion by small extremist parties; shamelessly open political bribery; blatant and obsessive partisanship by the nation's top policymakers; complete disregard for matters of national interest, such as the state of the economy or the absorption of Soviet Jews; and cynical and paternalistic attitudes toward the Israeli public. What was special about the 1990 spring crisis was that it happened on a larger and more intense scale. The spiritual gurus of the ultraorthodox parties – anti-Zionist rabbis in their eighties and nineties – were made the ultimate judges of Israel's national interest. Hundreds of millions of government dollars were readily committed as coalition bribery to tiny parties. Top ministerial and bureaucratic positions were offered to inexperienced and corrupt MKs in exchange for their votes. Several especially unscrupulous MKs used the opportunity to split from their mother parties, instantly tripling and quadrupling their price in the political supermarket. . . . *Pure proportionality has tended to produce not pure democracy, but its opposite: narrow, militant, forces holding the country hostage to their demands, not only in the formation of a government, but in the threat to bring it down if this or that legislation is passed.*[7]

Attempts at Reform

The manifest and blatant deficiencies in the functioning of the political system led to a major public outcry for radical reform of the constitutional, electoral and parliamentary systems.

Attempts to reform the extreme proportional representation (PR) system, as described in **chapter 3**, began soon after the establishment of the state. Many reforms were proposed, commencing with David Ben-

Gurion's proposal to replace the nation-wide party-list PR system with a simple-majority (winner-takes-all) system, based on the British model of single-member constituencies. Many proposals followed, such as one that would have increased the legal threshold from 1 to 10 percent. Another suggestion was for a multi-member constituency PR system – a mixed two-tier constituency nation-wide PR system whereby 90 MKs would be elected from 18 five-member constituencies and the remaining 30 MKs would be elected from a central list. This was tabled by the Labor Party in 1972 as a private member's bill, and it even passed the preliminary reading by the required minimum majority of 61 Knesset members. But the bill did not proceed to a first reading.

Electoral reform was almost the *raison d'être* of the Democratic Movement for Change Party, established in 1977. The October 1977 agreement, which brought this party into the coalition formed by Menachem Begin, stipulated that a proportional multi-member constituency system should be adopted. However, despite the fact that more than three-quarters of the members of the Ninth Knesset (1977–81) represented parties committed to electoral reform, no concrete steps were taken.

In July 1984, the Eleventh Knesset comprised members of 15 political parties. Neither of the two major blocs – the Labor Alignment and the Likud – could form a viable coalition, a patent result of the extremely divisive nature of Israel's electoral system. Moreover, the desire for reform was reflected later in the opinion polls: in 1965, only 29 percent of the public wanted to change the system, but by 1987, the proportion had risen to 69 percent.[8] In view of this impressive public support, 44 MKs from both the coalition and opposition parties decided to collaborate in order to present a private member's bill to amend the existing electoral system. Their proposed legislation was referred to the Constitution, Law and Justice Committee of the Knesset for a first reading, but it stopped there.

In September 1987, a group of professors from the Faculty of Law at Tel Aviv University recommended a mixed electoral system as part of their proposed constitution for the State of Israel. Their proposal was based on the principles of the West German electoral system (they were examining these principles and adapting them to the Israeli situation before the re-unification of Germany). They recommended that Israel be divided into 60 single-member constituencies and that the representatives be elected by a simple-majority vote. The remaining 60 Knesset members would be elected from a nation-wide list. There would be a 2.5 percent threshold, and successful parties would receive the number of seats proportional to their electoral strength, minus the number of seats they gained in the constituencies.[9] For instance, if a party obtained 50 percent of the total vote and won 40 seats in the constituencies, it would be entitled to 20 additional seats from the central list.

In addition to the changing of the electoral system, the Tel Aviv professors proposed a second very important reform, the adoption of a written constitution, including a bill of rights, based on the blueprint of their unsolicited proposed constitution for the State of Israel. They also proposed a third major reform, direct election of the prime minister, which actually meant a transition from the existing parliamentary system to a mixed premier–parliamentary system.

The professors realized that their proposal to reform the electoral system stood no chance of being passed in the Knesset because of the staunch opposition from the small and medium-sized parties, mainly the religious parties. Also, most of the incumbent MKs and professional politicians feared that any change in the electoral system rules would jeopardize their chances for re-election. There was strong objection, mainly from the religious parties, to the enactment of a secular, written constitution, including a bill of rights. The group of professors, who had established a popular grassroots movement called the Public Committee for a Constitution for Israel, reverted to the third major reform in their proposed constitution, namely, the direct election of the prime minister.

Consequently, four members of different parties agreed to combine their four different private member's bills into one, calling for direct election of the prime minister. After much deliberation and bickering among the members of the Constitution, Law and Justice Committee and in the Knesset plenum, the bill was finally approved by a vote of 55 to 23, on 18 March 1992.[10]

The main purpose of the demand for reform by the voluntary organizations was to strengthen the executive branch of the government by granting the prime minister the power to form a stable and effective government. This goal had the enthusiastic support of a large majority of the public. A petition for governmental reform was signed by over half a million citizens, and polls showed that almost 80 percent of the Israeli population supported direct elections.[11] In their efforts to strengthen executive power by proposing the direct election of the prime minister, the reformers actually brought about a major change in the parliamentary system, instead of just reforming the electoral system. Why was this reform successful when almost half a century of continuous effort to change the electoral system had failed?

We may discern a number of reasons to explain the success of the proposed reform of the political system. The reformers believed that the new system would free the prime minister from the extortionist demands of small parties and individual MKs when forming a cabinet. Furthermore, direct election would bestow upon the prime minister the legitimacy of a popular mandate to form a government quickly and effectively, within the framework of the existing parliamentary system. At the same time, the Knesset would continue to be elected by the prevailing proportional–nation-wide party-list system favored by the small parties.

The Labor Party's support of the new system was based on the belief that only a change in the pure parliamentary system would bring the party back to power, an assumption based mainly on two contentions: (1) the religious parties, which held a pivotal position in the formation of any coalition after the breakdown of the national unity government in 1990, tended to support the hawkish Likud, rather than dovish Labor; thus, only the direct election of a Labor candidate as prime minister would force them into a coalition with the Labor Party; and (2) the contest between two secular contenders, one a Likud candidate and the other from Labor, would, it was assumed, minimize the objections of the religious voters to a Labor contender because they would have no strong preferences in choosing between two non-religious candidates. On the other hand, the Arab votes cast for a Labor candidate would strengthen his chances of being elected. Although the Arab parties had supported Rabin's government without participating in his coalition, within the parliamentary system the Arab parties were not considered as legitimate partners to join the government.

Finally, the proposal for the direct election of the prime minister by a popular vote did not pose a threat to the party leadership's chances of being elected to the Knesset, since they had to choose only one candidate to head the Knesset list and thus did not jeopardize their own political fortunes. Furthermore, they had to do this even within the framework of the former parliamentary system. As Doron observes, "The reform was conceived as concerning only the apex of the pyramid, and therefore the risk of politicians supporting this reform was minimal."[12]

The New Premier–Parliamentary System

The provisions of the new Basic Law: The Government,[13] which came into effect beginning with the elections to the Fourteenth Knesset (1996), set out the legal framework of the new premier–parliamentary system. According to this Basic Law, the prime minister serves by virtue of his being elected in the national general elections, conducted on a direct, equal, and secret basis. The ministers are appointed by the prime minister, but their appointment requires the Knesset's approval. If the Knesset rejects the prime minister's proposals on the composition of his government, it is regarded as an expression of no-confidence in him, and he is dismissed from office. If this happens, the Knesset, too, is dissolved, and new elections for both the prime minister and the Knesset must be held within 60 days. This is also the case if the Knesset fails to approve the budget within three months of its submission to the Knesset.

Elections of MKs and of the prime minister are held on the same day, unless the prime minister is dismissed from office, is impeached for an offense involving moral turpitude, is removed from office by a vote of 80 of 120 MKs, resigns, is incapacitated, dies, or ceases to function as an MK. In all the aforementioned cases, special elections are held, and the newly elected prime minister serves in office until the termination of the Knesset's term.

A candidate is eligible for the prime ministership if he is 30 years of age, heads his party list and is a candidate for the Knesset, and his candidacy is supported either by a faction of the outgoing Knesset of no less than 10 members or by 50,000 enfranchised persons.

The provision that a candidate for the prime ministership has to be a member of the Knesset has been recently amended.[14] The amendment stipulates that if special elections are held (namely elections for the prime minister, but not for the Knesset) a candidate is eligible for the prime ministership even if he is not a member of the Knesset. This amendment was passed in order to enable Mr. Benjamin Netanyahu, who resigned his seat in the Fifteenth Knesset after his defeat by Mr. Barak in the elections of 1999, to enter the contest as a candidate for the prime ministership in the early special elections called by prime minister Barak in December 2000, after being in office for just one and a half years. In spite of the fact that the Basic Law was amended, Mr. Netanyahu changed his mind and decided not to run due to the fact that his demand that the Knesset also dissolve itself, and the elections be held both for the prime minister and the Knesset, was rejected. This amendment further weakens the position of the Knesset vis-à-vis the executive.

In order to be elected, a candidate must receive a majority of the votes, that is, at least one more than 50 percent of the votes. If no candidate receives a majority, run-off elections will be held two weeks after the publication of the results of the first elections. In the second round, only the two top contenders are entitled to participate, and the candidate receiving the larger number of valid votes will be chosen as the prime minister.

To balance the power granted to the Knesset to oust the prime minister by a vote of no-confidence supported by at least 61 members, and in order to prevent a situation of continuous deadlock when a majority in the

Knesset opposes the government, thus preventing its effective functioning, the law grants the prime minister the power to dissolve the Knesset. To exercise this power, however, the prime minister needs the approval of the president (a titular head of state elected by the Knesset). Another important provision states that the government shall not exceed 18 members in number or contain less than eight.

Before the enactment of the new Basic Law, there was no legal limit on the maximum size of the government. Thus, in order to satisfy the demands of various coalition partners, often the number of ministers exceeded twenty, incurring excessive public expenditure and damaging the government's effective functioning. However, this provision has been amended in order to enable Prime Minister Ehud Barak to strengthen the basis of his coalition by including more parties in order to accommodate their demands. The new amendment sets only the minimal size of the government, and stipulates that the number of ministers should not be less than eight.[15] Thus again coalition constraints dictate the number of ministers serving in the government.

The Basic Law enhances the power of the prime minister, making him first above unequals. He determines and changes the roles of his ministers; he may transfer powers and duties, unspecified in the law, from one minister to another; and he is authorized to establish government offices or abolish them, and unite or divide them. The prime minister may establish permanent or temporary ministerial committees, and may transfer to one minister powers that had been granted by law to another minister. He conducts the functioning of the government and sets out its working and voting procedures. The prime minister is granted an additional vote should a government vote be tied.

In view of the increased powers of the prime minister and the government, there are provisions in the Basic Law that enhance the Knesset's powers in some important matters. The Knesset is granted supervision of subsidiary legislation and greater control over the declaration of a state of emergency.

Since the establishment of the state, the Knesset has been empowered to declare a state of emergency, but the new Basic Law stipulates that the state of emergency must not exceed one year, unless it is renewed by the Knesset. The Knesset may at any time revoke a state of emergency. Emergency regulations enacted by the government expire three months after their enactment, unless extended by the Knesset. The government must also notify the Knesset Foreign Affairs and Security Committee should it decide to declare war. The powers of the Knesset committees have also been enhanced, with respect to requesting ministers and civil servants to appear before them and to provide the committees with information on request.

Hence the model set out in the Basic Law establishes a new system of government that is neither presidential nor parliamentary but premier–parliamentary. It is not presidential because, as Sartori points out, a presidential system is defined by three criteria: (1) the head of state (president) receives office by popular election; (2) during pre-established tenure, the head of state cannot be discharged by parliamentary vote; and (3) this individual heads the government or governments appointed.[16]

The premier–parliamentary system maintains two of Sartori's criteria defining a presidential system (the first and the third criteria), but contrary to the second criteria, the prime minister in a premier–parliamentary system can be discharged by a parliamentary vote of no-confidence by an absolute majority of 61 of the 120 Knesset members, or can be removed from office by a qualified majority of 80 members of the Knesset. Thus the prime minister in a premier–parliamentary system is dependent for survival on the support of party and coalition partners. Therefore, the premier–parliamentary system may be defined by four criteria:

1   The head of government (the prime minister), but not the head of state, receives office by popular election.
2   He heads the government or governments that he appoints.
3   He may be removed from office by parliament by an absolute majority (50 percent plus one vote), which also requires the dissolution of parliament, or by a two-thirds majority, which requires a new election of the prime minister but not the parliament.
4   He is dependent on the support of his party and that of his coalition partners in the parliament.

The Deficiencies of the Premier–Parliamentary System

When analyzing the consequences of the new system, one has to ask whether it meets the expectations of its proponents, that is, whether it strengthens the prime minister in order to establish a more stable, effective government. The growing empirical evidence seems to suggest that this is not the case.

The major deficiency of the premier–parliamentary system stems from the different principles by which the prime minister and the Knesset are elected. The prime minister is elected on the basis of a majoritarian formula, whereby he has to attain an absolute majority of votes in either the first or the second round of elections. The Knesset, however, is elected on the basis of a proportional formula, whereby the number of seats in the Knesset allocated to each party is determined by the proportion of the votes it receives from the electorate.

The combination of these two contradictory principles is like mixing fire and water and therefore yields drastically different results at the two levels of government: the prime ministerial (executive) level and the parliamentary (legislative) level. The expectations of the proponents of the new system were that the majoritarian formula would nurture and promote a more moderate candidate and would increase the centripetal tendencies in the party system, since the candidates for premiership would be compelled to moderate their agenda in order to appeal to the maximum number of voters. On the contrary, the split-ticket voting method resulted in extreme fractionalization of the Knesset. According to the new system, the voter was entitled to vote for one of the two candidates representing the two major parties and, at the same time, to cast a vote for a list of candidates of another party to the Knesset. Consequently, the power of parties representing sectarian interests has increased significantly.

The religious parties, which in no previous election received more than 18 seats in the Knesset, won 23 seats (almost 20 percent of the total Knesset seats in 1996). The two Arab lists almost doubled their representation from 5 seats in 1992 to 9 in 1996. Two new parties, Israel B'aliya (a party of new immigrants from the former Soviet Union) and the Third Road (established to oppose any withdrawal from the Golan Heights) won 7 and 4 seats, respectively, thus together attaining a pivotal role in any future coalition.

On the other hand, the representation of the two major parties declined drastically. The number of Labor MKs decreased from 44 in 1992 to 34 in 1996, and that of the Likud from 40 MKs in 1992 to 32 in 1996. Bearing in mind the integrative role that parties play in a political system, this was a serious blow to the government's political stability. This situation reoccurred with even more dramatic consequences in the elections of the Fifteenth Knesset in 1999, where the representation of the two largest parties dwindled from 66 seats in 1996 to a bare 45: Labor – by now called Israel One – elected 26 members, and the Likud 19 members.

The proponents of the new reform hoped to release the prime minister from the tedious business of forming and maintaining his coalition government. The new system, however, significantly increased the bargaining power of the small, medium-sized, and religious parties. First, as a candidate, the prime minister in the 1996 elections had to make concessions to the Ultra-Orthodox Degel Ha-Tora Party by promising its leaders the Ministry of Housing, a promise he fulfilled after his election. Furthermore, in order to be elected in the first round, the Likud candidate (Benjamin Netanyahu) had to guarantee 10 safe seats on the Likud Knesset list, five to Rafael Eitan, the leader of Tzomet, a right-of-center party, and five to David Levi, the head of the new Gesher Party, a group of former Likud members who decided to leave the party.

These guarantees were to ensure that Eitan and Levi gave up on their declared intention to run for prime minister. Without the support of followers of Tzomet and the Gesher Party, Netanyahu had no chance of being elected. The new electoral winner-takes-all formula caused Netanyahu to reduce drastically the number of Likud members on its Knesset list in order to make room for his new Tzomet and Gesher partners.

The second phenomenon reoccurred when Barak, as the Labor candidate, had to safeguard in his new Israel One party two seats for Gesher candidates (David Levi and his brother) and a seat for Rabbi Malchior, one of the leaders of Meimad – a moderate Orthodox party. Thus after the defection of Levi from Barak's coalition the number of seats held by Israel One decreased from 26 to 24.

After being elected, Netanyahu once again had to negotiate a coalition agreement with his partners, as in the "good old days" of the previous parliamentary system. He had to yield to pressures from his own party to appoint to his cabinet ministers he did not want. He had to create a new Ministry of National Resources to appease a leading member of his party, and he had to make significant concessions to his coalition partners (Gesher, the Third Road, Israel B'aliya, and the religious parties) in order to pass his first budget in the Knesset. A group of MKs from his own and other coalition parties formed a lobby threatening to vote no-confidence in the prime minister should he decide to make concessions on issues such as the unity of Jerusalem, the return to Syria of the Golan Heights, and the West Bank settlements. The same was the fate of Barak after the elections to the Fifteenth Knesset. As Arian predicted, the prime minister, within the framework of the premier–parliamentary system, would have to pay more in terms of his own time to calm his coalition partners, and more in terms of the national budget to keep the coalition together.[17]

In view of the grave shortcomings of the new system, a public outcry ensued, supported by a growing number of MKs from both the Labor and the Likud parties, to abolish the new Basic Law, or at least to amend article 19 so that a vote of no-confidence by 61 Knesset members would require the election of a new prime minister without, at the same time, necessitating the dissolution of the Knesset.

Conclusion

One can pronounce a definite verdict on the functioning of the new premier–parliamentary system, after successive failures of two prime ministers to maintain a stable and effective government and both PMs having to call for early elections in a period of four years (1996–2000).

The attempt to impose decisions made by a prime minister, elected by a bare majority (as in the case of Netanyahu, who won the elections by a majority of 50.4 percent of the total vote) in a deeply divided Israeli society with a fragmented and polarized party system, is destined to fail. As Mainwaring points out, in multi-party presidential systems, the ill functioning of the system is due to the fact that the president cannot find sufficient support in a multi-party system requiring a consensus among the parties in order to form a sufficient majority to support the policies of the president.[18]

The same applies to Barak even though he won the 1999 elections with an impressive support of 56 percent of the electorate. Subsequently he could not find sufficient support for his government in the Knesset. Indeed, the presidential systems based, as in the premier–parliamentary system, on the election of the chief executive on the basis of a majoritarian principle perform very poorly, with the sole exception of the United States.[19]

The empirical evidence favors the parliamentary model in general, and it favors this model for divided societies in particular. According to Bingham Powell and Bayliss, the parliamentary model is superior to presidential government in controlling violence, in encouraging participation in economic growth, and in limiting inflation, unemployment and strike activity.[20] Hence, retaining the parliamentary system as a part of the premier–parliamentary model was right. However, in order to overcome the major deficiencies that characterized the Israeli parliamentary system, as explained earlier in this chapter, some reforms of the pure parliamentary model became necessary.

According to Sartori, the most successful systems are semi-presidential (as in France and Finland) or premiership systems (as in England and Germany). Furthermore, he states, "My stance is [that] semi-presidentialism can improve presidentialism; similarly . . . semi-parliamentary systems (if I may so call the Kanzler or premiership formula) are better than plain parliamentary ones."[21]

It seems to me that once Israel decided to abandon its plain parliamentary system, it should have opted for a slightly amended Kanzler formula rather than the unique and unprecedented premier–parliamentary system. The Kanzler system is based on two principles: (1) that the candidate of the largest party winning the election automatically becomes prime minister; and (2) the "constructive no-confidence" formula, namely, that the prime minister (the *Kanzler*) cannot be removed from office by the parliament (the *Bundestag*), unless the initiators of the vote of no-confidence can produce, at the same time, an alternative candidate supported by an absolute majority in the parliament.

The adoption in Israel of the principle of the constructive vote of no-confidence would guarantee that the prime minister could not be removed from office unless an alternative candidate enjoying the support of an alternative majority of Knesset members was re-elected in his place.

However, the adoption of the principle of the Kanzler model, which stipulates that the leader of the largest party that wins in the elections immediately becomes prime minister, would deter the small and medium-sized parties from supporting such a reform in Israel because it would threaten their very existence or significantly weaken them. Therefore, my proposal is that the leader of the party winning the largest number of seats in the elections would be called on to form the government within 15 days. Failing to do so, the leader of the second-largest party would be given 15 days to accomplish this task. This would, on the one hand, allow the small and medium-sized parties to have a say in the process of coalition formation, but, on the other hand, it would force them to decide within 30 days which party they wanted to join, since it is highly improbable that they would agree to call for new elections 30 days after the previous elections.

Thus the two important elements of the slightly amended Kanzler model would strengthen the position of the prime minister in the forming and maintaining of a stable coalition government, within the framework of the parliamentary system which is best suited for a deeply divided society such as Israel, in which the only viable model of decision making is a consensus model.

5

The Knesset as a Representative Assembly

Among the four main functions of the parliament – (1) legislation, including financial legislation; (2) checking and controlling of the executive; (3) providing legitimacy to the government's actions; and (4) representation – the representative function of the Knesset was drastically affected by the new electoral law of the direct election of the prime minister. In this chapter I shall analyze the impact of the new electoral law on one aspect of representation – passive or microcosmic representation – in the representational function of the Knesset. I am assuming that instead of increasing the stability and effectiveness of the government, as was the aim of the initiators of the new electoral law for the direct election of the prime minister, it increased representativeness, which caused even greater fractionalization of the Knesset, further undermining the stability and effective functioning of the government.

Of the many ambiguous concepts related to democracy, perhaps none is more ambiguous than the concept of representation. Although the concept has been at the very heart of democratic theory, political scientists admit that "in spite of many centuries of theoretical effort, we cannot say what representation is".[1] It has been noted that this ambiguity stems from the very nature of the concept: "representation, taken generally, means the making present in some sense of something which is nevertheless not present literally or in fact. Now, to say something is both present and not present is to utter a paradox, and thus a fundamental dualism is built into the meaning of representation . . . ".[2]

While more meanings of the term may be pointed out, it seems that in operational terms (and thus in the perspective of researchability) the essential distinction is that between "active" (or responsible) representation and "passive" (or sociological) representation.[3] According to Mosher, in cases of active representation "an individual . . . is expected to press for the interests and desires of whom he is presumed to represent, whether they be the whole people, or some segment of the people", while passive representation deals with "the source of origin of individuals and the degree to which, collectively, they mirror the total society . . . ".[4] Returning to Eulau's previously quoted remark,[5] it may be said that indeed we do not know what "active representation" is, nor do we know exactly the nature of the connection of the links (direct or indirect, i.e., through intervening variables) between active and passive representation.[6] However, we do know a great deal about measurable passive representation.

Admittedly, then, passive representation may be researchable, but it covers only a part, and perhaps a relatively less illuminating part, of the subject as a whole. Nevertheless, passive representation yields important information about the nature of a given political system. It is highly unlikely that in any political system we would find social forces represented in the political elite in the same proportion as their numerical strength in the population. Nor does classic democratic theory (as distinct from certain contemporary trends of thought) presume that this must be the case. It follows that over-representation and under-representation (together, misrepresentation) are likely to be found in just about all political systems.

Passive representation and misrepresentation fulfill important functions in politics. Representation increases the status of social forces (in their own eyes as well as in those of others); it helps legitimize the political system and the rules of the political game; it indicates the sources and criteria of political recruitment; it makes probable that given perspectives will be considered in making decisions;[7] it reflects upon those political institutions (e.g., the legislative branches of government) which have at least partial representative function; it provides visible and measurable criteria of social change; and it describes the social bases of politics. These functions are perceived by political reformers, who often emphasize remedying misrepresentation as an essential and, in fact, central ingredient of reform. Hence, reformers frequently argue for a quota system in manning various political offices, because the quotas ensure representation of under-privileged groups in some proportion to their numerical strength, at least as a temporary measure. In this chapter I am not concerned with the question as to whether or to what extent a parliament should represent the various demographic or socioeconomic groups in a society, i.e., to what extent it should fulfill what Sartori defines as the "nominal-representative function" of the society.[8] Rather, I am interested in the over- and under-representation of social groups in the Knesset insofar as the representation

74

is indicative of the power and prestige structure of the society. MKs are still regarded (in spite of the diminution of power of the parliament) as an important part of the political elite. Thus, the over- or under-representation of major social groups tells us a great deal about the distribution of power, prestige and influence in a political system. Moreover, many political scientists interested in representation believe that, ideally, elected representatives should be similar to their electors so that the assembly is a social microcosm of the nation. It is worthwhile to quote Birch on this matter:

> Advocates of this view have suggested that an assembly cannot be properly representative of the nation if its social composition is *conspicuously* different from that of the electorate. In homogeneous societies such as Britain this kind of argument, though often used as a basis for criticizing existing institutions, has rarely cut much ice, *but in societies divided on social or religious lines its impact has naturally been much greater.*[9]

In order to examine the changes in the representational functions of the Knesset I have analyzed the changes in the social, political and cultural background of the Knesset members – from the inception of the Knesset in 1949 and until the Fifteenth Knesset, which was elected in 1999 – a period of 50 years.

The variables chosen to analyze the changes in the composition of the Knesset (i.e., the passive aspects of representation) were the following: gender, age, ethnic origin (Ashkenazi or Sephardic), national origin (Jews and Arabs), religion (religious Jews and secular Jews), place of residence and regional residence. In order to measure the under- and over-representation of the various groups and sectors in the Knesset, the following index of misrepresentation is used:

$$R = \frac{C-E}{E}$$

Where:
R is the index of misrepresentation.
C is the percentage of Knesset members belonging to a certain demographic category.
E is the percentage of a demographic group belonging to the same category among eligible voters.

I decided to use the ratio of a demographic group among eligible voters, and not among the total population of a given demographic group, because

I think it's more relevant since it represents the maximum electoral potential of a demographic group.

Thus (–1) means "non-representation", (+1) means "over-representation", and (0.0) means "perfect representation".

The main findings

The data in tables 5.1 and 5.2 demonstrate that the under-representation of the oriental Jews (Sephardic) in the Knesset almost disappeared. While in the First Knesset in 1949, the MKs of oriental origin comprised 2.5 percent, in the Fourteenth Knesset their representation increased to 36.7 percent, and 35.6 percent in the Fifteenth Knesset. In terms of our index of under-representation, in 1949 it indicates (–0.92) – close to total non-representation, while in the Fourteenth and Fifteenth Knessets the index shows almost perfect representation (–0.07) and (–0.06 respectively). Thus, since the introduction of the direct election of the prime minister in 1996 the percentage of Sephardic MKs has increased significantly, namely by 7.1 percent, and reached almost perfect representation.

This impressive increase in the passive representation of the Sephardic Jews in the Knesset may be explained by the distinct rise in the representation of the Ultra-Orthodox Sephardic Shas party from six MKs in the Thirteenth Knesset to 17 MKs in the Fifteenth Knesset, due mainly to the introduction of the split-ticket vote.

In terms of national origin, we witness also an impressive increase in the representation of non-Jews (Arabs). The MKs of Arab origin comprised 3.1 percent of the total number of the First Knesset in 1949, while in the Fourteenth Knesset their number had almost tripled to 9.1 percent. It continued to increase, to 10.8 percent. Once again, the split-ticket voting encouraged the establishment of new parties in the Arab sector, increasing the number of the MKs belonging to the Arab sector by 4.1 percent, since the 1992 elections.

In terms of the index of under-representation we witness a substantial decrease in the under-representation of the Arab sector, from (–0.77) in the First Knesset to (–0.25) in the Fourteenth Knesset. In the Fifteenth Knesset the representation of the MKs of Arab origin continued to increase and reached 10.8 percent of the total number of MKs in the Knesset. The index of under-representation shows almost a perfect representation (–0.14) of the Arab sector in the Fifteenth Knesset.

In terms of religiousness the percentage of Orthodox and Ultra-Orthodox Jews in the Knesset also increased significantly, from 12.2 percent in the First Knesset to 19.2 in the Fourteenth, and to 22.5 percent

Table 5.1 Frequencies (in percentages) of main demographic variables in terms of Knesset seats (K1–K15: 1949–1999)

Variable	Values	1999 K15	1996 K14	1992 K13	1988 K12	1984 K11	1981 K10	1977 K9	1973 K8	1969 K7	1965 K6	1961 K5	1959 K4	1955 K3	1951 K2	1949 K1
Gender	Male	88.3	92.5	90.8	94.2	91.7	93.3	93.3	91.0	93.3	92.1	91.1	91.7	90.4	90.6	90.6
	Female	11.7	7.5	9.2	5.8	8.3	6.7	6.7	9.0	6.7	7.9	8.9	8.3	9.6	9.4	9.4
Age	21–40	7.5	14.2	15.0	13.3	11.7	8.3	12.5	16.0	8.9	6.5	8.2	8.8	12.7	20.9	20.5
	41–60	77.5	73.3	70.0	65.0	71.7	75.0	67.5	58.0	61.9	71.8	68.7	73.6	72.4	66.7	64.6
	61+	15.0	12.5	15.0	21.7	16.7	16.7	20.0	26.0	29.2	21.7	23.1	17.6	14.9	18.4	14.9
Ethnic origin	Ashkenzim	52.4	54.2	59.2	64.2	66.7	73.3	78.3	87.0	89.2	89.2	95.0	93.7	95.0	96.7	97.5
	Sephardim	36.8	36.7	34.2	30.8	27.5	22.5	15.8	13.0	10.8	10.8	5.0	6.3	5.0	3.3	2.5
National origin	Jews	89.2	90.9	93.3	95.0	94.2	95.8	94.2	96.9	96.5	96.2	96.5	96.1	95.6	95.3	96.9
	Non-Jews	10.8	9.1	6.7	5.0	5.8	4.2	5.8	3.1	3.5	3.8	3.5	3.9	4.4	4.7	3.1
Religion	Religious	22.5	19.2	13.3	15.0	10.8	10.8	14.2	12.1	14.7	14.0	15.4	18.5	13.8	15.9	12.2
	Secular	77.5	80.8	86.7	85.0	89.2	89.2	85.8	87.9	85.3	86.0	84.6	81.5	86.2	84.1	87.8
Place of residence	City	78.3	70.8	73.3	73.3	75.8	77.5	*	81.5	75.4	78.6	76.5	76.7	71.1	78.9	76.1
	DT#	5.8	11.7	10.0	9.2	6.7	5.8	*	1.8	3.4	0.9	1.7	0.9	1.7	*	*
	Kibbutz	4.1	6.7	5.0	5.8	7.5	6.7	*	11.5	16.1	15.4	17.4	17.2	22.8	16.7	19.6
	Other rural	11.8	10.8	11.6	11.6	10.0	10.0	*	5.2	5.1	5.1	4.4	5.2	4.4	4.4	4.3
Region of residence	North	10.0	17.5	13.3	10.8	10.8	9.2	*	*	*	*	*	*	*	*	*
	South	18.3	13.3	13.3	11.7	10.0	9.2	*	*	*	*	*	*	*	*	*
	Central	29.3	15.0	15.0	10.0	10.8	12.5	*	*	*	*	*	*	*	*	*
	Tel Aviv	12.5	21.7	30.8	35.0	32.5	42.5	*	*	*	*	*	*	*	*	*
	Haifa	3.3	7.5	6.7	7.5	11.7	9.2	*	*	*	*	*	*	*	*	*
	Jerusalem	22.5	18.3	17.5	22.5	22.5	16.7	*	*	*	*	*	*	*	*	*
	JSG ***	4.1	6.7	3.3	2.5	1.7	0.8	*	*	*	*	*	*	*	*	*

* Data not available
\# Developing towns
*** Judea, Samaria & Gaza

Table 5.2 Representation measures for the main demographic variables in terms of Knesset Seats (K1–K15: 1949–1999)

Variable	Values	1999 K15	1996 K14	1992 K13	1988 K12	1984 K11	1981 K10	1977 K9	1973 K8	1969 K7	1965 K6	1961 K5	1959 K4	1955 K3	1951 K2	1949 K1
Gender	Man	0.77	0.85	0.82	0.88	0.83	0.87	0.87	0.82	0.87	0.84	0.82	0.83	0.80	0.81	0.81
	Woman	-0.77	-0.85	-0.82	-0.88	-0.83	-0.87	-0.87	-0.82	-0.87	-0.84	-0.82	-0.83	-0.80	-0.81	-0.81
Age	21–40	-0.82	-0.73	-0.77	-0.81	-0.83	-0.86	-0.77	*	-0.66	-0.71	-0.69	-0.68	-0.55	-0.36	-0.50
	41–60	1.28	1.57	1.46	1.44	1.64	1.78	1.40	*	1.91	2.24	2.11	2.32	2.27	2.03	2.14
	61+	-0.34	-0.34	-0.11	0.22	0.08	-0.08	0.12	*	0.39	0.07	0.22	-0.01	-0.03	0.26	0.15
Ethnic origin#	Sephardim	-0.06	-0.07	-0.18	-0.31	-0.37	-0.47	-0.61	-0.74	-0.78	-0.78	-0.89	-0.86	-0.89	-0.92	-0.92
	Ashkenzim	0.15	0.21	0.28	0.47	0.47	0.55	0.63	0.74	0.76	0.73	0.78	0.74	0.70	0.62	0.44
National origin	Jews	0.02	0.08	0.06	0.08	0.96	0.06	0.04	0.14	0.13	0.09	0.09	0.08	0.08	0.72	0.12
	Non-Jews	-0.14	-0.25	-0.44	-0.58	-0.47	-0.58	-0.37	-0.79	-0.76	-0.67	-0.69	-0.65	-0.60	-0.57	-0.77
Place of residence	City	}-0.08**	-0.10**{	-0.11	-0.11	-0.09	-0.07	*	*	0.03	0.14	0.09	0.15	0.11	0.24	0.18
	DT##			0.02	0.00	-0.28	-0.37	*	*	-0.79	-0.95	-0.88	-0.95	-0.86	-1.00	-1.00
	Kibbutz	0.65	1.79	0.79	0.87	1.42	1.23	*	*	3.76	3.39	3.43	3.11	3.66	2.41	1.88
	Other rural	0.96	-0.86	1.23	1.19	1.08	1.13	*	*	-0.32	-0.37	-0.61	-0.60	-0.77	-0.76	-0.59
Region of residence	North	-0.23	0.13	-0.14	-0.28	-0.26	-0.34	*	*	*	*	*	*	*	*	*
	South	0.14	0.06	0.10	-0.01	-0.15	-0.20	*	*	*	*	*	*	*	*	*
	Central	0.54	-0.31	-0.31	-0.53	-0.48	-0.38	*	*	*	*	*	*	*	*	*
	Tel Aviv	-0.51	-0.07	0.17	0.27	0.12	0.42	*	*	*	*	*	*	*	*	*
	Haifa	-0.80	-0.46	-0.54	-0.49	-0.23	-0.41	*	*	*	*	*	*	*	*	*
	Jerusalem	0.73	0.68	1.01	1.56	1.62	0.96	*	*	*	*	*	*	*	*	*
	JSG###	0.15	2.53	1.36	1.50	3.25	1.67	*	*	*	*	*	*	*	*	*

* Data not available.

** The exact number of residence in developing towns during the election days was not availabe. Therefore, we refer to the representation measure for cities and developing towns together.

\# Dat on ethnic origin of the population are based on formal publication of the elections results. Since no other information was available we assumed that 50% of thos who were born in Israel were Askenazim and the other 50% Separdim.

Developing towns.

Judea, Samaria, & Gaza.

in the Fifteenth Knesset. The new electoral system was again a major deter-
minant in the unprecedented increase in the representation of the Orthodox
and Ultra-Orthodox Jews in the Knesset. The percentage of MKs in this
category grew by 9.2 percent following the introduction of the split-ticket
system, mainly due to the increase in the representation of Shas, which is
not only a Sephardic party, but also an Ultra-Orthodox religious party.

The most misrepresented social category are women. Their representation declined from 9.4 percent in the First Knesset (1949) to
7.5 percent in the Fourteenth Knesset (1996). The index of under-
representation increased from (−0.81) in the First Knesset to (−0.85) in the
Fourteenth Knesset. The percentage of women slightly increased to 11.7
percent in the Fifteenth Knesset, and consequently the index of misrepresentation of women in this Knesset decreased to (−0.79). The slight
improvement in the representation of women is due mainly to the policy of
affirmative action undertaken by some parties which introduced a limited
quota for women on the "safe seats" of their lists of candidates. This
slight improvement in the representation of women cannot be attributed to
the introduction of the split-ticket voting. It has much deeper social,
political and cultural roots. Its roots relate to some of the major social
cleavages dividing Israeli society. In this regard there are three major cleavages effecting the representation of women: the religious and secular
cleavage, Jews and Arabs, and Sephardic and Ashkenazi Jews. These
three cleavages have a distinct impact upon the representation of women
in the political system. The Orthodox Jews, comprising about 20 percent
of the population and maintaining close to 25 percent of the seats in the
Knesset, reject the very notion of women's participation in the political
process. The more moderately orthodox NRP has granted a symbolic
representation to women from time to time, but it is unrealistic to expect
that an Orthodox Jew who prays every morning "Blessed be He that did
not create me as woman" would support the election of women to the
Knesset.

The Arab sector, which comprises about 18 percent of the population
and whose share in the electorate is about 12 percent, has also a traditional
negative attitude toward the participation of women in political life. Part
of the Sephardic sector, which comprises more than one-half of the Jewish
population and close to one-half of the electorate, also has a traditional
outlook that views women's participation in politics unfavorably. Herzog
found that 60 percent of the activists in the Center of Herut (the ruling body
of the Likud), as against 34 percent in the Center of the Labor Party
(the party center is the ruling body of the party), regard themselves as
observant Jews, which also may explain partly the small number of women

elected on the Likud list to the Knesset.[10] Hence, the social structure of Israeli society creates an unfavorable "climate of opinion" towards the participation of women in politics.

A major political factor having great impact upon the representation of women in the political system is related to the fact that Israel has been in a state of war with most of its Arab neighbors since its inception as a sovereign state in 1948. Security and the maintenance of a strong army are the salient issues in Israeli politics. The security problem of Israel is regarded as of overriding importance by both men and women, deferring any other consideration including the demand for a greater representation of women in politics.

The Israeli case defies most of the accepted explanations prevailing in the literature outlining the most important factors facilitating an increase of the representation of women in parliament. According to common wisdom, Israel's extreme PR list system with a very large district magnitude and a low threshold, and with an average turnover of one-third of its Knesset members, should have brought about the election of an impressive number of women.[11] Yet, as we have shown, the number of women elected to the Knesset is small.

It seems to us that the impact of the electoral system (chiefly the district magnitude) on the extent of the representation of women is very significant in single-member constituencies. In PR multi-member constituencies, the district magnitude is an important factor, but more significant are the cultural, socioeconomic and political factors, which should be explained individually for each country.

The number of women in the Knesset would increase if more women were willing to run for higher political office and if women's organizations within and outside political parties were to unite to support more female candidates, both financially and organizationally. One must bear in mind that women in Israel enter politics at a later age and thus lack political experience and visibility.

Paradoxically, democratization of the nomination system by the introduction of primaries in the Labor Party and the decision of the Likud to introduce primaries in the elections to the Fourteenth Knesset resulted in a decline of women's representation in the Knesset because primaries reduce the legitimacy of introducing quotas. Similarly, democratization of the electoral system, by introducing a multi-member constituency system with a preferential vote enabling a choice of two or three district candidates, would also most probably decrease the chances of women to get elected unless the initiators of the proposed electoral reform would agree to increase the district magnitude to at least five or more.

Since in Israel the Knesset is elected on the basis of a single country-wide district of 120 members, and not on the basis of geographical constituencies, the electoral system has only a very limited influence on the MKs' residential and regional aspects of representation. Moreover, there are no national parties organized on the basis of local-interest representation.

Thus, although the kibbutzim comprise about 2.5 percent of the total population their rather distinct over-representation from 1.88 in the First Knesset to 0.65 in the Fifteenth Knesset stems from the historic mission the kibbutz movement played in the establishment of the state, and in the organizational resources they still provide to the Labor bloc in terms of volunteers and transportation facilities during the election campaign and on the election day.

The emphasis of the sectorial rather than the district aspect of representation within the country-wide PR list system vindicates itself in the almost continuous under-representation of the Northern district and mainly the Haifa district (−0.23) and (−0.80) respectively.

The over-representation of the Jerusalem district is due to the city's status as capital of the country and the seat of the Government and the Knesset. It may also be indicative of the professionalization of the legislative role, since a number of veteran Knesset members have moved their residence to Jerusalem during their long-term service in the Knesset.

The rather significant improvement in the representation of the developmental towns and the Southern district is due mainly to the increase in the number of MKs of Sephardic origin. In analyzing the profile of the MKs on the basis of Pearson's (r) correlation test according to the variables of age, gender, ethnic origin, religiosity, education, place of residence, turnover and the number of years as MKs in the Knesset, I have found that Jewish MKs who come from the periphery are usually younger, of oriental origin, with a lower education and fewer years of service in the Knesset than their counterparts (see table 5.3).

Thus, although the introduction of the split-ticket voting system, upon which the premier–parliamentary system is based, improved to a large extent the "passive" representative function of the Knesset, it had a negative impact upon the stability and effective functioning of the government. The increase in the "mirroring" function of the Knesset enhanced its fractionalization and fragmentation, thus impairing the stability and effectiveness of the government.

Instead of the ill-fated governmental reform, probably the most needed structural reform is in the realm of changing the rigid country-wide proportional-list system. A reform in this sphere might bring about a change not only in the passive (sociological) sense of representation, but

Table 5.3 Correlation matrix (Pearson's r) for the researched variables (1977–1999)

Variable	N	Mean	S.D.	1	2	3	4	5	6	7	8
1. Age	840	51.31	9.17	–							
2. Gender	840	.08	.27	.05	–						
3. Origin	783	.70	.46	.27	.10**	–					
4. Ethnicity	840	.14	.12	-.11**	.04	.02	–				
5. Religion	840	.15	.36	-.04	-.11**	-.22**	-.05	–			
6. Education	829	.62	.49	-.12**	-.01	.16**	.03	-.04	–		
7. Residence area	746	.51	.50	.12**	.10**	.15**	-.13**	0.05	.14	–	
8. Turnover	840	.35	.48	-.27**	-.02	-.05	.04	.06	-.02	-.06	–
9. Years in Parliament	840	6.80	7.70	.54**	-.03	-.06	-.06	.02	-.02	.05	-.60**

N = Number of Knesset Members

* P<.05

** P<.01

also in the active (responsible) representation, by attracting into the political process new groups which so far have been reluctant to take part, and by diversifying the profile of the potential pool of candidates for legislative and cabinet posts.

A change in the direction of a proportional electoral-*constituency* system, which would put more emphasis on the personality of the candidate and would increase the influence of the local branches in the process of selection, would consequently tend to attract more independent candidates and to increase the chances of candidates with better educational and professional qualifications. It would make for a more balanced representation by adding the territorial principle to the present sole principle of sectorial representation.

It would possibly result in a more stable and effective government by mitigating the extreme fractionalizing and polarizing effect of the sectorial character of representation stemming from the country-wide PR list electoral system to the Knesset.

6

Proposals for Presidential Government in Israel

In spite of the fact that the direct election of the prime minister was introduced in 1996 there are still those who believe that the adoption of a presidential system in Israel will bring about the establishment of a stable and effective government capable of dealing successfully with the major problems that face Israel.[1] Moreover, the personality of the President would, they claim, become a symbol of national unity; it would help to reduce the major cleavages dividing Israeli society, namely between the religious and secular sectors, between Sephardic and Ashkenazi Jews, between Jews and Arabs, rich and poor, doves and hawks. The necessity of establishing a coalition government is singled out as the major deficiency of the present premier–parliamentary system. The proposals to change the premier–parliamentary system would put an end to the almost extortionist character of the demands made by the minor coalition parties on the government. These pressures, according to the proponents of the reform, have been the main factors in undermining the stability of the government, and its ability to govern; these factors create major anomalies in the allocation of scarce national resources.

The presidential system, essentially like that of the Fifth French Republic, is singled out as particularly relevant to remove the shortcomings of the Israeli political system.

The Conceptual Framework

Western democracies share a common philosophical tradition based on a number of principles originating in the social and political revolutions of the seventeenth and eighteenth centuries. Among these principles, the concept of a separation of powers with built-in checks and balances, the idea that political power should be accessible to every citizen, and the sanctity of the basic rights of the individual to life, liberty and equality before the law, comprise the core of the fundamental ideology of the western democratic tradition.

The operational components of the fundamental ideology – such as constitutions, electoral systems, party alignments and patterns of leadership, and centrally the interaction among them – determine the main institutional arrangements prevailing in western democracies, namely the two-party cabinet system; the multi-party parliamentary system; the presidential system and the quasi-presidential system of the Fifth French Republic,[2] as well as the *régime d'assemblée*, which existed under the Fourth French Republic.

It is our assumption that the institutional framework within which a democratic government operates and the prevailing political culture have a major impact upon the behavioral determinants such as stability, effectiveness, representativeness, responsiveness and accountability of the political system.

Figure 6.1 presents the fundamental and operational principles, and the structural and behavioral components, on which the major patterns of government are based.

We believe that it is timely to deal with a neglected area of political science, circumscribed by the following questions: (1) Under what circumstances and for what reasons does a need for change in a governmental system arise? (2) What are the conditions necessary for a successful change? (3) Is it feasible to transfer a system of government from one political environment into another? (4) What are the probable costs and benefits of such a transference?

In this chapter we shall limit ourselves to questions 2 and 4, namely the consideration of the changes needed in the operational components in order to bring about the major change in the institutional structures, and the costs and benefits of such a change. The cost–benefit analysis will help us to consider the desirability and the price, in terms of advantages and disadvantages of such a change. The multi-party parliamentary system of Israel will serve as a case study for our discussion.

In principle we argue that the quest for stability, effectiveness, legitimacy and the implementation of effective checks on governmental activities is the major drive motivating those who call for a radical change in the institutional setup of a democratic political system. However, the patterns of government in western democracies are very stable and the chances of changing, let us say, a multi-party parliamentary

Figure 6.1

1. FUNDAMENTAL PRINCIPLES	Separation of Power
	Decentralization of Political Power
	Basic Rights of the Individuals

2. OPERATIONAL COMPONENTS	Constitutions
	Electoral Systems
	Party Alignments
	Patterns of Leadership

3. INSTITUTIONAL PATTERNS OF GOVERNMENT	The quasi Presidential System	The Presidential System	The Régime d'Assemblée	The Multi Party Parliamentary System	Two-Party Cabinet System

4. BEHAVIOURAL VARIABLES	Stability
	Effectiveness
	Representativeness
	Responsiveness
	Accountability

system into a two-party cabinet system or a presidential system are negligible.

The transformation of the *régime d'assemblée* in France into a quasi-presidential system in 1958 is probably the only example of a major change in the institutional patterns of a democratic system, following the Second World War, aside from the quite unsuccessful attempts at an institutional transference of western patterns of government into the newly established states of the Third World.[3]

It seems to me that the development of a major crisis – such as an outbreak of war, an imminent threat of a military coup, a major economic or social crisis, an acute conflict within the governing elite, or a threat by anti-establishment or extra-parliamentary groups to the legitimacy of the existing government – is a necessary condition for the implementation of a major institutional reform. However, even an acute crisis would not always be followed by a major institutional reform.

Crotty suggests that "the reform cycle follows a general pattern which can be divided into four stages: the problem, the crisis, the reform and the reaction".[4] Contrary to Crotty's concept of reform as a four-step process, we suggest that a crisis would not necessarily be followed by reform if a drastic decline in the legitimacy of an existing government is successfully resolved by a change in government or by the establishment of a wall-to-wall coalition.

In a sharply fragmented society such as Israel, a consensus over the establishment of a wall-to-wall coalition is preferred over a major institutional reform with all its uncertainties and risks to the present political establishment, which would include the main coalition and opposition parties.

A case in point are major crises developed in the 1980s, namely the 1982 Lebanese débâcle, and the 1983 collapse of the Stock Exchange leading to the 1984 elections stalemate, which resulted in neither the Likud nor Labor being able to form a government. Consequently both blocs preferred a wall-to-wall coalition, over the introduction of major reforms in the electoral or parliamentary system.

We would thus further argue that whenever a major institutional reform is successful, as in the case of France, its success depends upon a significant change in the four structural components of a political system, namely the constitution, the electoral system, the party system, and the patterns of leadership.

A constitutional change is necessary in order to establish a legal framework for the new institutions and to set up the formal provisions that defend the rule of law and the rights of citizens. In a multi-party system a change in the electoral law of the parliament is imperative, to drastically reduce the number of parties, so as to enable the establishment of a stable government. Finally, charismatic leadership is required in order to facilitate an orderly transfer of government and the effective functioning of the new regime.

On the other hand, the main factor which makes a change in the pattern of government very difficult is the cultural context of legitimacy within which a political system operates. As Laski observed in his well-known exchange with Price on presidential and parliamentary systems:

> I am . . . in no way seeking to eulogize the parliamentary system at the expense of the presidential or vice versa; each seems to me to have its own special

merits, and neither is likely to be capable of transference to another environment where alien traditions are deeply rooted, without becoming something very different from what it was in the country of its origin . . . [5]

Thus for a multi-party parliamentary system with a number of significant and deep-rooted cleavages, an attempt to impose greater stability and effectiveness at the expense of representativeness may end up in a major crisis of legitimacy. This, in turn, could lead to the alienation of some important groups, and to the formation of outer parliamentary protest movements which would endanger the very foundation of the democratic system. A situation such as this did not develop in France because, during the existence of the Third Republic, the French had used for a long time a majoritarian electoral run-off system, which gives far less representative results than the proportional representation system prevailing in Israel. Moreover, the change in the French parliamentary system in 1958 occurred as a result of an imminent threat of a military coup d'état, and the transition to a presidential system was facilitated by the emergence of de Gaulle's charismatic leadership. None of these conditions applies to the Israeli case, at least under the present circumstances.

The reform of the direct election of the prime minister was adopted in 1992: it established a new and unique premier–parliamentary system in Israel. It occurred in spite of the lack of the aforesaid conditions, because it did not change the electoral system of the parliament (the Knesset), which continues to be elected on the basis of an almost pure proportional representation (PR) system. Moreover, the split-ticket voting under the premier–parliamentary electoral system, whereby the prime minister was elected on the basis of a majority two-ballot system and the Knesset by a country-wide PR list system, brings about even a much greater representation of the major cleavages dividing the Israeli society in the Knesset.[6] The transformation of the parliamentary system into a premier–parliamentary system became possible due to the fact that it required a change only in the apex of the system – the election of the prime minister – and thus did not jeopardize the political careers of members of the parliament. As a result, it was relatively easy to obtain a consensus on the direct election of the prime minister, whom the aspirants for a parliamentary career would have to elect even within the framework of the parliamentary system.

Finally, the limitation of the reform of the direct election of the prime minister alone, without changing the electoral system to the Knesset, became a major factor in the malfunctioning of the present premier–parliamentary system as discussed in **chapter 4**. Due to the acute problem of governability after the establishment of a new premier–parliamentary system it is highly probable that this hybrid model would not survive for long and would be replaced by some kind of a parliamentary system, most probably of the German-type Kanzler system.

Moreover, in a recent study[7] Rahat argues that the success of the reform which established the direct election of the prime minsister was due to specific factors characterizing the Israeli case, such as the involvement of a significant number of non-governmental interest groups and voluntary organizations, and the fact that the reform movement started under the popular banner demanding the promulgation of a formal constitution.

According to Rahat, the more decentralized the process of a political reform becomes and the more widespread the involvement of civil groups which dissociate themselves from politicians and parties, the more chance there is of reform being accepted.

The main thesis presented in this chapter is that those who advocate adoption of the presidential system in Israel on the ground that a more stable and effective government would result are seriously mistaken on three points:

1   the nature of the American and French presidential systems;
2   the changes in the operational components needed to establish similar systems; and
3   the probable negative consequences of such a reform in the Israeli context, because of the high value attached to representativeness in its political culture and tradition.

The Israeli Setting

Contrary to the common notion that the Israeli parliamentary system has been weak and unstable, it is our contention that, with some reservations to be discussed later, it contained some impressive features of a stable and strong system. The average duration of a cabinet, since the establishment of the state, has been close to two and a half years, a record which compares favorably with that of most western parliamentary democracies.[8] The average duration of the parliament, elected for a term of four years, has been 3.5 years. Even more important, although the religious parties have participated in almost all the coalition governments since 1949, they have played a pivotal role in the coalition in only seven out of the eighteen cabinets, serving from 1949 until 1977.[9] In all other cabinets during this period, the Labor Party could rely on a left, right or centrist coalition. Moreover, during this period the "status quo" agreement applying to religious issues was respected by both the religious and secular parties.[10] Thus, after the elections to the Second Knesset in 1951, there were only a few crises over religious matters. The influence of the religious parties, mainly that of Agudat Yisrael, became dominant only after the access to power of the Likud in 1977; the issue became more acute after the elections of the Tenth Knesset in 1981, when Agudat Yisrael attained the position of a party pivotal to the coalition.

Moreover, in terms of effectiveness, and subject to the agreed upon coalition program, the powers of the Israeli government in both foreign and domestic matters were impressive. In the realm of foreign affairs, the cabinet had the power to declare war without the consent of the Knesset and to conduct war without proper consultation with its Foreign and Defense Relations Committee. The cabinet had the power to carry out its foreign and defense policy, without any serious impediments posed by the opposition. In the realm of domestic affairs the government was the prime initiator of both financial and regular legislation. The Knesset had only limited control over the budget and no power to change it. The government had the power to issue by-laws and thousands of regulations were issued without proper and effective control by the Knesset. An emergency regulation may alter any law, suspend its effect or modify it, and may also impose or increase taxes or other obligatory payments.[11]

The political system in Israel is a highly centralized one, lacking effective checks and balances. There are no sub-governments as in a federal system. Although the High Court of Justice occupies a respected position in the defense of civil and individual rights, it has no power of judicial review. There is no second chamber to restrain the lower house of the government. Israel has no formal constitution and, with very few exceptions, a law can be passed by a simple majority, by the Knesset. As long as the government enjoys a majority in the Knesset, parliament has limited control and influence on the government. There was a continuous public complaint about insufficient participation of its members in plenary sessions and the activities of the committees. The committees had no real powers, such as being able to subpoena witnesses or to compel members of the government to appear before them. Party discipline was strong and the voters' influence on their representatives was nil. This was mainly due to the nature of the electoral system of the Knesset, which is a country-wide proportional-list system.

In the framework of the parliamentry system the main institutional constraint restricting, in any significant way, the power of the government was its coalition bonds. However, the necessity to establish a coalition government has occasionally had a serious impact upon the stability of the government and its ability to govern. Thus small ideological parties such as Tehiya and Tami in the coalition governments of Begin and Shamir, and, most significantly, the religious parties, particularly Agudat Yisrael, have held the balance of power in the government. As Felsenthal points out, "in small coalitions, small parties are overpaid . . . ".[12] Moreover we would argue that, whenever small sectarian parties play a pivotal role in a coalition, the high payoffs that the majority has to concede in order to maintain coalition bring about a serious distortion in the allocation of natural resources, and pose a continuous threat to the very ability of the government to survive.

It is therefore imperative that any change in the present constitutional framework, such as proposed by the advocates of a major political reform, on the one hand, would guarantee the stability and effectiveness of the executive branch but, on the other hand, would create institutional constraints at least co-equal to the checks and balances maintained by the present coalition arrangements.

It is our contention that neither the American nor the French presidential systems would fulfill both of the above-mentioned conditions in the Israeli circumstances.

The Applicability of the American System

The main appeal of the American system to the Israeli reformers stems from the stability of the President's term in office. It is based on the belief that a stable four-year term will liberate the prime minister from the fetters of his coalition partners. It is claimed that it would enable the PM to stand up firmly against excessive demands of coalition partners, as they would be unable to jeopardize the existence of the government. However, while it is true that the tenure of the American President is safeguarded by the Constitution – except in the very exceptional and rare case of impeachment – his is not necessarily an office of effective and responsible leadership. As Rose points out, "the great challenge in America has been to create effective government".[13]

The position of a chief executive in the Israeli environment would become even more problematic than in the United States. He might survive in office, but at the expense of exercising effective leadership. Most probably his party would not enjoy a majority in the Knesset and, once again, he would become dependent on a coalition or even face a solid, well-disciplined opposition which would paralyze his ability to act – as we have witnessed in the collapse of PM Barak's coalition (January 2001), compelling him to declare special elections just one and a half years after his election. Thus a stalemate would be likely to characterize a presidential system in Israel.

Moreover, the structure of the American government is entirely different from that of Israel. The American system is based on a written constitution; Israel has no formal constitution. America has a simple-majority single-member district system with its natural tendency toward a two-party system; Israel has adopted the proportional representational list system, which encourages the multiplicity of parties. America has a loose pragmatic two-party system, while Israel has a cohesive, more disciplined and ideologically oriented party system. Moreover, the United States has a federal system of government with a multitude of sub-national governments, while Israel has an extremely centralized unitary system of government. Thus, the adoption of the American system in Israel would require a very radical change in the structure of the Israeli political system. It would require the adoption of a formal constitution, a radical change in the electoral system, and a decentralization of the administrative and bureaucratic structures and functions of government.

Functionally, the American system, contrary to the parliamentary system, is based on a more pronounced notion of the separation of powers, as well as checks and balances. It is based on the Founding Fathers' fundamental distrust of any form of strong government or strong political parties. Their aim was not to establish a powerful and effective executive, but, on the contrary, to check and restrain the executive in the most effective way. The Congress has the power to hinder the policies of the President and "this state of institutional belligerency makes it next to impossible . . . to establish policy goals, and reach them".[14] Even though the power of the federal government has expanded in recent years, as reflected in the proliferation of programs and agencies, the ability of the President to manage and direct the government apparatus has not been commensurate with his responsibilities. This has created a situation whereby "some of the excesses of imperial presidential leadership seem to have been attempts to flail out at the very aspects of the political environment that make the presidency a potentially stalemate institution".[15] Thus, although the separation of powers has not prevented a strong president from accruing power, it impedes the responsible exercise of power by either the executive or the legislative branch. Ultimately the power of the President rests mainly in his ability to persuade, his skills in bargaining with the various interest groups and his willingness to compromise.[16] Hence while the expectations of presidential performance are high, the capacity of presidents to live up to those expectations is low.[17]

Thus it is clear that the American system of government does not provide for an effective, cohesive and responsible type of government, as expected by those who favor its adoption in Israel.

If the American presidential system does not fit Israeli circumstances perhaps the French system might.

The Applicability of the French System

The presidential system of the Gaullist type is rooted in a much more similar tradition to that of the Israeli parliamentary system than is the American. The Fifth Republic was established on the ruins of the parliamentary system of the Fourth Republic. It has retained some of the important features of parliamentary government in that the prime minister and the cabinet are responsible to the National Assembly and obliged to resign when the Assembly succeeds in passing a vote of no-confidence in the government. The principle of collective responsibility before parliament is, of course, a basic characteristic of the parliamentary system in Israel. Furthermore, France and Israel have a multi-party system reflecting some of the basic cleavages dividing their respective societies, and both are unitary and highly centralized political systems. Moreover, France is the only western-type democracy where a parliamentary system has been superseded by a presidential system. Thus it presents a unique case from which we can learn about the preconditions of change from one pattern of govemmental system to another.

However, here the similarities and usefulness of the Gaullist model with regard to its possible application to the Israeli context end. The French changed their parliamentary system into a presidential system because the parliament was too strong and the executive branch too weak, while in the Israeli case the executive is quite strong and the legislature quite weak. To strengthen the executive, the French introduced a number of important provisions in the constitution of the Fifth Republic: The president appoints the prime minister, who is responsible both to him and to the Assembly. The president has the right to dissolve parliament, to declare a state of emergency (which entitles him to use widespread emergency powers), to call for a referendum through his prime minister and to initiate both financial and regular legislation.[18]

In Israel the prime minister enjoys most of the powers granted to the French president. He has the right to issue emergency regulations, although he needs the consent of the cabinet for this purpose. At the very least, the emergency powers of the Israeli prime minister and the government are greater than those of the French president, since Israel is still in a state of emergency.[19] The prime minister of Israel and the government are the prime initiators of financial and regular legislation. The prime minister has the right to dissolve parliament; his resignation requires the resignation of the cabinet and thus might cause the dissolution of parliament. Hence many provisions aimed at strengthening the power of the executive in France have long been an integral part of the unwritten Israeli constitution. Why then, despite the similarity in the powers of the Israeli prime minister and the French president, has the new French system seemed to provide France with a much more vigorous and effective leadership? The reason, it seems to me, stems from the fact that the transition from the parliamentary to the presidential system in France was accompanied by a number of reforms which provided the necessary conditions for the establishment of stable and effective government. Reflecting on the parliamentary system of the Fourth Republic, Michel Debré commented: "the political divisions of France were created by the parliamentary system. Parliament is not the legitimate expression of the nation . . . but only a product of a particular electoral system and of a constitution approved by only one-third of the electorate, of which one half were communists".[20] Thus two major reforms were imperative: the change of the constitution and the change of the electoral system, which in turn had a major impact upon the party system.

The Promulgation of a New Constitution

The 1946 Constitution was replaced by de Gaulle in 1958 with a new constitution in order to establish a legal framework for the institutions of the New Republic. As the chief arehitect of the new constitution remarked: "To achieve unity, a strong executive, a state with authority, France needed new institutions."[21] The new constitution significantly increased the powers of the executive, but it also contained a number of guarantees to safeguard the rule of law and the rights of citizens.

As Bogdanor points out: "It is perhaps no coincidence that the Fifth Republic which has seen the growth of coherent majorities has also seen the development of a form of judicial review by the Constitutional Council, an important modification of traditional French doctrines of the sovereignty of Parliament."[22]

In Israel, however, the process of constitution-making began fifty years ago and has not yet been completed. It is highly improbable that a transition to a presidential system would somehow miraculously bring an end to the opposition, mainly of the religious parties, and bring about a secular constitution. Thus it seems to me that in Israel an increase in the powers of the executive branch, within the framework of the presidential system, would not be checked and balanced by a written constitution, as witnessed by the inability of the "Constitution for Israel" movement to convince the Knesset and the Israeli public to legislate a formal constitution.[23]

The Change of the Electoral System of the Parliament

The transition to the presidential system in France involved changing the electoral system. The proportional representation system introduced in 1946 was replaced by a majoritarian system with *two ballots*. The new electoral system has helped the ruling party to obtain a clear majority in parliament, thus providing the president with solid support in the Assembly.

As Goldey and Williams note: "A real proportional system would surely have deprived the UNR (the Gaullist party) of its dominant position in the Assembly, and given the Communists closer to eighty seats than the ten they actually won, for the clear discrimination in favour of the former and against the latter was much magnified on the second round."[24] Moreover, they convincingly argue that the two-ballot system in France was a necessary even though not a sufficient condition of political recovery between 1958 and 1962.[25]

In Israel the present practice of electing the Knesset on the basis of a country-wide, proportional representation list system has been the subject of debate since the establishment of the state. The continuous and strenuous objection of the small parties and even party blocs, mainly of the religious parties, to a reform of the electoral system, stemming from their fear that a change in the present proportional representation system would significantly diminish their representation in the parliament and weaken their bargaining power within a coalition government, make any major change in the electoral system improbable in the foreseeable future.[26] However, without a change in the electoral system of the Knesset, it is very likely that the elected president would face the same fragmentation in the parliament as the prime minister faces under the present parliamentary system and, as a result, would be unable to gain the necessary parliamentary support for his policies. On the other hand, if the impossible happened and the electoral system of the Knesset were to be changed, should the president's party fail to win a clear majority in the parliament, he might face a united, cohesive, well-organized, ideologically-oriented and well-disciplined opposition which would undermine his ability to govern.

If my argument is correct, the introduction of a presidential system of either the American or the French type in Israel would not bring about the hoped-for results, namely, the creation of a more stable and effective government. What is needed in order to establish a more stable and effective government in Israel is not a change of the parliamentary system, but a reform of the electoral system of the Knesset, which would bring about a decrease in the number of parties. In addition the promulgation of a formal constitution is necessary in order to institutionalize the "rules of the game" and provide for more effective safeguards of the basic rights of Israeli citizens. But is the realization of such a reform feasible?

The Feasibility of Adopting a Major Reform in the Electoral System of the Knesset

The opposition to any serious reform of the electoral system of the Knesset stems from the fact that Israel is a highly politicized society.[27] The stakes in gaining control over the government are so great and the fear of losing power so intense that neither of the major blocs – the Likud or the Labor Alignment – is prepared to agree on a major reform of the electoral system of the Knesset.

In this respect the Israeli case is not unique. The same situation prevailed in Austria after the end of the Second World War when, according to Engelmann, one of the chief reasons for the continuation of the coalition between the two major blocs – the Socialists and Catholics – stemmed from "the heritage of the 'lager' situation, which expressed itself in the fear of both subcultures of being governed by the other".[28] In the Israeli case both party blocs are prepared to accept the burdens of the present loose coalition system, as it serves as the most effective restraint on the governing party on the one hand, and provides the opposition with the best chance to topple the government on the other. And it enables them to resort to the establishment of a wall-to-wall coalition whenever a major crisis occurs.

A second factor presenting great difficulty in introducing serious reform has to do with the vested interests of the politicians and party functionaries in preserving the present system. A fundamental change in the rules of the political game may jeopardize the power positions held by the present political elite. That elite opposes any proposal to change the prevailing system.

Finally, the persistent objection of the religious parties to a major reform makes any attempt to change practically impossible. The adoption of the presidential system or a major change in the electoral system of the Knesset would significantly weaken the bargaining power of the religious parties, and therefore makes any serious change in the present electoral system of the Knesset almost unthinkable.

Concluding Remarks

It seems to me that the present coalition system in Israel reflects basic social cleavages; it is deeply rooted in the pre- and post-state tradition of the country. Therefore, instead of trying to supersede the coalition system by adopting a new pattern of government, it would be more realistic and advisable to introduce some middle-range institutional reforms that would reduce the occasionally negative impact of small but pivotal coalition partners on the stability of the government. What are some of the preconditions necessary to carry out such institutional reform in Israel?

Perhaps the most important precondition is to reduce the pervasive influence of politics that penetrates the whole fabric of Israeli society. In this connection some middle-range institutional reforms such as a drastic limitation of the electoral campaign from the present duration of several months to twenty-one or thirty days would be useful. But perhaps the most important reform in this regard should be the formation of a depoliticized civil service based on merit and not on political appointments. The establishment of a school similar to the ENA (Ecole' National d'Administration) in France would be a most salutary step toward the education and training of such an administrative elite.

However, in the short term, a moderate reform of the electoral system that would increase the barrier for electing a member to the Knesset from 1.5 percent to 4 percent would have a salutary stabilizing effect by probably reducing the number of parties in the Knesset from fifteen, at present, to about five or six, thus mitigating the social cleavages. A 4 percent barrier would probably lead to the formation of three major blocs: the Labor Alignment, the Likud and a Religious bloc. Three small parties, the Communist, a centrist and a right-wing party, might also get representation in the Knesset. The new party configuration might bring about the establishment of either a Labor–Center or a Likud–Conservative coalition with the Religious bloc serving as an important, but not necessarily a pivotal partner, in the coalition.

In the long run, a significantly greater stability and effectiveness of the government would be achieved only upon the resolution or reduction of some of the major cleavages dividing Israeli society. As Goldey and Williams point out, the new form of government in France succeeded in establishing "stable, effective, majoritarian government, acceptable to the nation" predominantly because "long-term developments in French society were simplifying the political scene by reducing the number of cleavages".[29]

The Political Consequences of Direct Elections of the Prime Minister and the Heads of Local Councils: A Comparison between Local and National Levels

A comparison of the election of the prime minister at the national level, and the heads of local authorities at the local level, enables us to compare the political consequences of this system when applied at the two different levels of government. At both levels, the national and the local, the electoral system is similar – in principle almost identical. It is comprised of a majority two-ballots system in the election of the prime minister and the heads of local authorities, and a PR list system in that of the local councils and the Knesset. The only difference is that in the direct elections of the prime minister a second ballot is conducted if no candidate received at least 50 percent +1 vote, while in the case of local authorities, a candidate is elected on the first ballot if he obtains at least 40 percent +1 vote.[1]

The deviation from the majoritarian principle of the requested 50 percent +1 vote in the first round in the elections of the heads of local authorities was introduced by the two major parties – Likud and Labor – in order to enable them to win most of the electoral contests already at the first ballot. Thus, in the recent local authorities elections in 1998, were the 50 percent + 1 principle adhered to, only 60 percent of the mayors would have been elected, while with the present requirement of a 40 percent + 1 threshold, 83 percent were elected. It would appear that this arrangement indeed works in favor of the largest parties.

The difference between the two systems in the elections for the Knesset and the local councils is in the different legal threshold applied at the two levels. Since the election of the Thirteenth Knesset in 1992, the legal threshold in the Knesset elections has been 1.5 percent of the total votes. In the elections to the local councils the legal threshold is calculated on the basis of a quota for each local authority. Hence the legal threshold varies according to the size of the local councils. In the large municipalities – such as Jerusalem, Tel Aviv and Haifa – that elect 31 members to the local council, the threshold is 2.4 percent, while in the small municipalities electing nine members to the council the legal threshold is 8.3 percent: exactly according to the rule applying to the magnitude of the district – in our case the size of the local council – the greater the magnitude of the district, the more proportional are the results.[2]

We shall now analyze the reasons for adopting the split-ticket majoritarian system in the election of the prime minister and the heads of the local authorities, and the PR method in the elections to the Knesset and local councils, and their impact on the stability and effectiveness of the government at the local and the national levels.

The main incentive of political reformers, on both local and national levels, stems from one of the major dilemmas in any democratic system – that of finding a proper solution for the implementation of the principles of both governability and representativeness, in order to establish a stable and effective government. The aim is to find a proper balance between these principles, because as a rule we can maintain that the more we enhance the principle of representativeness, the more we diminish governability and vice versa.

Thus, since the establishment of the State of Israel there has been an attempt to find the right combination of these two principles, mainly between the need to obtain stable and effective government, and at the same time to safeguard proper representation of the main social cleavages dividing Israeli society, both in the Knesset and in the local councils.

Both reforms, that for the election of the heads of local authorities, introduced in 1975, and the reform of the direct election of the prime minister introduced in 1992, were intended to increase governability and to decrease representativeness, which at present magnifies the fragmentation of Israeli society as reflected in the composition of the Knesset and the local councils.

The law requiring direct elections for the heads of local authorities indeed increased governability, by enhancing the status of the heads of local authorities, bestowing on them both the legitimacy of being directly elected by their residents, and the power granted to them by the new law increasing their authority. The purpose of the reform was also to enable the heads of local authorities to establish local coalitions without being compelled to yield to the excessive demands of their coalition partners.

The aim of the reform of direct election of the prime minister on the national level was also intended to increase governability in order to enhance the stability and effective functioning of the national government. The new electoral system was aimed to shorten the period of coalition formation, and to enable the elected prime minister to establish stable coalitions, without having to surrender to the sometimes extortionate demands of small and medium-sized parties, mainly from the religious sector.

In analyzing the political consequences of both reforms we would argue that while reform at the local level succeeded in achieving a more stable and effective government, at the national level it failed in these respects.

The electoral system, which is based, on both the national and local levels, on the system of split-ticket voting, in itself carries the seeds of division and fragmentation of the political system, because it enables the voter to vote for a candidate of one party in the elections for the prime minister, or the head of a local authority, and for a list of candidates of a different party in the elections to the Knesset or the local councils.

In a deeply divided society like Israel, such an electoral system magnifies the magnitude of fractionalization in the assembly, whether it is the Knesset at the national level or the (local council) municipality at the local level.

However, the fragmentation and fractionalization created by the new electoral system has a different impact on the national level than on the local level, for the following reasons:

1 Although the local authorities perform an important task in supplying services, and allocating valuable resources that have a significant impact on our way of life, they are not involved in dealing with the ideological and existential problems, such as war and peace, which divide Israeli society. Therefore, a candidate seeking the premiership is prepared to pay any price in terms of allocating material resources or offices in order to obtain the maximum support of the voters, even if he greatly weakens his party's representation in the Knesset or in the local council. Thus the candidate of the Likud in the 1996 election campaign, Mr. Netanyahu, had to sacrifice ten seats on the Likud party list to the representatives of two right-of-center parties (Gesher and Tzomet), in order to preclude the possibility of their respective leaders contesting the elections, thus dividing the right-of-center bloc and almost certainly endangering his election as prime minister. The leader of the Labor Party, Mr. Barak, had to use the same tactics, sacrificing three seats on his list to two small parties (Gesher and

Meimad) in the 1999 elections. Thus, in order to form a stable coalition, the prime minister has to sacrifice the interests of his party in order to be elected.

2   The local government depends heavily on the central government in two major respects: a great part of the local government's budget derives from the central government. The minister of the interior has the power to dismiss a local authority head, and, if he sees fit, to dissolve the council in a case where the local authority is unable to provide the basic services to its inhabitants, or if the head of the local authority behaves extremely irresponsibly in handling his municipality's financial matters. In distinct contradiction, on the national level, the law dealing with the direct election of the prime minister placed great impediments in the process of his dismissal, and even makes it close to impossible. In order to depose the prime minister from office, a two-thirds majority (80 out of the 120 MKs) is required.

Moreover, the premier–parliamentary system based on the principle of the direct elections of the PM prohibited any possibility of replacing the PM, within the legal term of his office, even if he becomes a "lame duck". It also prohibited making basic changes in the policies of the prime minister and his government. Contrary to the premier–parliamentary system, within the framework of the parliamentary system prevailing in Israel until 1996, it was possible to replace the PM by means of his own party, and to change or modify his coalition, or the policies of his government, without having to use the rather paralyzing and costly measure of conducting new elections before the expiration of the legal term of the Knesset. Thus, again, the stability and effectiveness of the government is seriously impaired.

3   The weakening of the ties between the local branches of the national parties, and the impressive increase in the number of independent local parties, has the positive effect of increasing the autonomy of local government. The drastic weakening of the two major parties (Labor attaining 26 seats, and the Likud 19) in the 1999 election due mainly to the fractionalizing nature of the split-ticket system, was seriously damaging to the stability of the national government because it undermined the integrative function of the national parties. The weakening of the parties' discipline and cohesiveness as a result of the new premier–parliamentary system had far more negative consequences for the stability of the government on the national level than on the local one.

4   The extreme fractionalizing effect of the new electoral system had much more serious consequences on the formation of coalitions at the national level than at the local level. At the local level, the power granted by law to the head of the local authority to maintain his office is safe-

guarded by his authority to use one-twelfth of his previous budget, even when the opposition and the local council does not allow him to pass a new budget, and thus enables him to stay in power until he manages to form a stable coalition. Hence, even though the new electoral system has brought about some instability in a number of local councils due to the fact that the mayor was unable to form a stable coalition for a period of time, this phenomenon is limited to a small number of local authorities.[3] On the contrary, at the national level, the acute problem of coalition building and maintenance has a serious effect on the ability of the national government to govern.

The results of the election to the Fourteenth and Fifteenth Knessets under the new electoral law reflects the major shortcomings of the new electoral system (the direct election of the prime minister) and these are summarized as follows:

1   The fragmentation of the party system increased and brought about fractionalization and polarization in the Knesset.
2   The support for the two major parties – the Labor Party and the Likud – dwindled to such an extent that it undermined the very possibility to establish a stable government. Both parties together polled just 34.4 percent of the votes (Labor 20.3% and Likud 14.1%) and thus neither was able to form a viable coalition.
3   The new electoral system made the Knesset members more independent of their parties and thus drastically reduced cohesiveness and party discipline in the Knesset. This situation greatly impaired the PM in his efforts to maintain a stable government.
4   The new electoral system significantly increased the bargaining power of small and medium-sized parties, and predominantly the religious parties. The PM under the new system was under constant pressure to surrender to the almost extortionist demands of these parties.

Contrary to the negative impact of the direct election of the PM at the national level upon the stability and effective functioning of the national government, the very same system has had quite a positive influence in improving the governability at the local level. We shall now summarize the positive influence of the direct elections of the heads of the local authorities at the local level:

1   The most impressive impact of the new system at the local level has been the immense increase in the power and attraction of the local parties. The local parties have more than quadrupled their representation in local

government since the introduction of the new electoral system in the local elections of 1978. In 1973 the independent parties polled less than 10 percent of the vote, while in the last local elections in 1998 their electoral support increased to 44 percent.[4] The increase in the strength of the local parties had a salutary effect at the local level reflecting the growing autonomy of the local government. It demonstrates the lessening influence of the national parties in local politics. The national parties are no more the omnipotent "King Makers" in nominating candidates and shaping the nature of local coalitions or setting the local agenda.

2   The legitimacy bestowed upon the heads of local government as a result of their direct election and the increased authority that the new law granted them has significantly improved their ability to govern and the stability of local government. It is true that in a number of localities the mayors face a "hostile council", i.e., a council in which the mayor has not been able to form at least a minimum winning coalition, but the status and powers which the new electoral system and the law expanding his authority granted him enable him to "muddle through" and ultimately to form a stable coalition.[5] There were only very few instances in which the Minister of the Interior had to dismiss a mayor and dissolve the council because the mayor could not function and was unable to provide even minimal services for residents.

3   The new electoral system intensified the process of the declining impact of ideology and national platforms at the local level. The issues in local government became more "localized" – the local agenda being set by local issues and not by party ideology.

4   The increased role of local parties and issues enhanced by the new electoral system played a major role in the transition of local government from an etatist and material culture, into a civic and post-material culture. The parties at the local level began to turn their attention from issues of *being* to issues of *well-being*.

Conclusions

In order to minimize the negative aspects of the electoral system in the direct elections of the heads of local authorities there is a need to reform also the PR list system in the elections to the local councils. As in the case of the heads of the local authorities there is a need to apply the same system, i.e., a direct election of the councils, on the basis of a majority two-ballot system in single-member districts based on the division of local authorities into a number of boroughs or precincts equaling the number of councilors elected to the local councils. In Israel, the number of councilors ranges from nine members in small local authorities to 31 members in the three largest cities.

Such a reform would achieve the following aims:

1   It will increase the autonomy of local government. The councilor would become the representative of his district directly responsible to the voters.

2   It will bestow upon the councilors the same legitimacy of being elected by the people of the local district, as is at present bestowed upon the heads of the local authorities.

3   The new electoral system of the local council would reduce the "Bonapartist" tendencies of the heads of local authorities, who are at the present the sole actors enjoying the legitimacy of being directly elected by the residents of their municipality. It would thus make for a more balanced division of power between the mayor and the local councils. Such a reform would also increase the responsibility and responsiveness of the councilors to the local electorate.

4   Finally, such a reform would further reduce and weaken the control of national parties and specific sectors on local government issues, since the national parties would not be able to aggregate votes from the locality at large as is the case under the present PR list system. Thus, for instance, the Ultra-Orthodox parties would not have been able to gain control of almost 50 percent of the 31 seats in the Jerusalem local council by the support of less than 20 percent of the electorate, because secular voters who constitute the majority in most of the neighborhoods of Jerusalem would not vote for an Ultra-Orthodox candidate in their district.

While at the local level the introduction of the majority two-ballot system also in the election of the local councils would further improve the stability and effectiveness of local government, at the national level a return to the previous parliamentary system with two important reforms is imperative. The two necessary reforms are the introduction of the constructive no-confidence formula guaranteeing that the prime minister cannot be removed from office unless an alternative candidate, enjoying the support of an alternative majority of Knesset members, is re-elected in his place. The second reform relates to the shortening of the process of coalition formation (see **chapter 4**). Both reforms are imperative in order to make for a more stable and effective government at the national level.

Concluding Remarks: Toward Electoral Reform

What can we learn from the Israeli experience about electoral engineering at the national and local levels? It is true that in the debate as to whether electoral systems are independent or dependent variables we are not dealing here with an intrinsic independence,[1] yet I would argue that in the Israeli case the cleavage structure of Israeli society is the determining factor in the impact upon the stability and effective functioning of the government.

The socioeconomic, ideological and religious cleavage structure was already deeply rooted in the *Yishuv* period and reflected in its extreme multi-party system. Since during the *Yishuv* period the Jewish community enjoyed authority without sovereignty,[2] the political system could function only within a broad consensus, and thus an extreme PR system was adopted.

The socioeconomic, ideological and religious cleavages were transferred to the newly established State of Israel since its inception in 1948. It is therefore no wonder that Louis Guttman[3] succeeded in classifying the Israeli parties by his (Guttman's) scale according to their stands on economic issues and the issues of nationalist policies from right to left, though he added the religious dimension as a second dimension.

However, since the Six Day War of 1967, in addition to the by now weakened left–right divide along the socioeconomic division, the ideological dimension became a major cleavage dividing the Israeli society between hawks and doves according to their attitude toward the Israeli-Arab conflict and the issue of settlements in the occupied territories. This cleavage was reinforced by the ethnic (Sephardic vs. Ashkenazi) and national (Jews vs. Israeli Arabs) cleavages, greatly affecting the stability and effective functioning of the government by turning the party system into a polarized, extreme multi-party system. Thus although the extreme

PR list country-wide electoral system did not cause the extreme fragmentation of the party system, it has definitely helped in maintaining it and as a result contributed to the destabilization and ill functioning of the political system.

The ideological cleavage in the aftermath of the Six Day War intensified the difference between right and left, and coupled with the débâcle of the Yom Kippur War, dramatically de-legitimized the rule of the Labor Party, bringing about a major change in the government resulting in the ascent of the Likud party as the leading party since the upheaval in the 1977 elections. However, Likud's role as the leading party lasted only from 1977 to 1984 when the election results brought about a tie between the two major blocs (Likud and Labor), necessitating the establishment of a National Unity government.

After the disruption of the consensus which united the National Unity government from 1984 until 1990, the stability and effective functioning of the government was fundamentally shaken. An outcry for radical constitutional, electoral and governmental reform became imminent and tumultuous.

Since the absence of a consensus to promulgate a formal constitution or to fundamentally reform the present electoral system failed (see **chapter 3**), the reformers, joined by now by civic and political groups,[4] succeeded in mobilizing the public and creating also a consensus among politicians to agree upon a governmental reform, that would establish a new and unique premier–parliamentary system (analyzed in **chapter 4**). However, the foundation of a new premier–parliamentary system having a multifaceted nature – namely the introduction of the split-ticket voting, i.e., a majority run-off system in the direct election of the prime minister while retaining the extreme PR country-wide system in the elections to the Knesset – proved counterproductive. Instead of creating a more stable and effective government it caused a further fractionalization and fragmentation of the party system, decreasing the representation of the two large parties and increasing significantly the representation of the small and sectorial parties in the Knesset (see chapter 5).

The proposals to adopt the presidential or semi-presidential system in the Israeli circumstances (see **chapter 6**) are hardly feasible since any major governmental reform is prone to face strenuous opposition because it contradicts the politicians' and party functionaries' vested interests in preserving the present system. Fundamental change in the rules of the political game may jeopardize the power positions held by the present political elite. In addition the persistent objection of the religious parties, holding a pivotal role in any government, to a major reform, makes any attempt to change the system practically impossible. The adoption of the presidential system or a major change in the electoral system would significantly weaken the bargaining power of the religious parties, and therefore makes any serious change in the political system almost unthinkable.

Only a resolution or a reduction of the two major cleavages – the ideological cleavage dividing Israelis between doves and hawks and the religious cleavages between Orthodox and secular Jews – may contribute to a significantly greater stability and effectiveness of the government.

The success of the reform on the local government level and its failure at the national government level (see **chapter 7**) points to the perils of deducing from the political consequences of political reform at the micro-local level to the macro-national level. Reform at the local level has been successful because of the centralized nature of the national government and its firm control of local government, and the decreasing interest of the national parties in local party affairs. This enabled the formation of a consensus among the two major parties, Labor and Likud, to institute the two-faceted reform at the local government level. Thus the stabilizing effect at the local level of government was not duplicated at the national level.

As Sartori points out, "the plain fact is that after 50 years of pure proportional representation, Israel must face the urgent need for an electoral reform that seeks efficient government and penalizes party atomization".[5] However, the pertinent question, as Lijphart points out, is "to what extent are politicians able and willing to manipulate the electoral system?"[6]

Analyzing the major proposals to reform the electoral system in Israel it seems to me that the only possibility to mobilize consensus among politicians for a reform of the electoral system is a mixed-constituency proportional system along the lines of dividing the country into fifteen districts, on the basis of the present administrative division of the country, and electing 60 MKs on a national at-large district in which adjustment seats would be allocated so that nation-wide proportionality is achieved. In order to ascertain the proportionality of the allocation of seats on both the district and national levels the Hare and LR formula should be adopted for both levels and as far as possible the legal threshold should be increased from the present 1.5 percent to 3 percent. Until the ideological and religious cleavages are reduced or resolved, only such a moderate reform is feasible in the Israeli circumstances. But even such a modest reform would contribute to the improvement of the stability and effective functioning of the Israeli political system. Dividing the country into fifteen district constituencies would strengthen the contacts between the MK and his or her constituency and make for a more responsible and responsive representation of the local groups and personal interests of the voters.

Introducing a preferential system would enable the voters to choose among candidates and thus eliminate the need to nominate the candidates for the Knesset on the basis of the primary system, which has a divisive influence on the functioning of the political system as a whole. It would also reduce to some extent the number of parties represented in the Knesset, and thus again make a salutary contribution in improving even in a moderate manner the stability and efficient functioning of the governmental system.

And to this end I endorse Lijphart's view that specific proposals for electoral reform need not be, and cannot be, drastic or radical, but should move toward "incremental improvements, not revolutionary upheaval, of existing systems".[7]

Postscript

Just as the book was going to press *The Basic Law: The Government*, on which the new premier–parliamentary system was established, was rescinded.[1] During the five years of the existence of the premier–parliamentary system (1996–2001) three prime ministers were directly elected: Benjamin Netanyahu in 1996, Ehud Barak in 1999, and Ariel Sharon in 2001.

The bitter experience of five years of chronic instability necessitating two early elections, in 1999 for both the Knesset and the prime minister, and in 2001 a special election of the prime minister only, came to an end.

The new Basic Law: The Government re-established the parliamentary system prevailing in Israel for almost 50 years, from 1949 until 1996. It is encouraging that the new *Basic Law: The Government* promulgated by the Knesset on 7 March 2001 abolished the premier–parliamentary system, and re-established the parliamentary system according to the principles proposed by the author of this book.

The new law includes amendments intended to cure the major deficiencies of the previous parliamentary system, namely the abolishment of the two-ballot system,[2] the establishment of a more definitive process for the formation of the government,[3] as well as the adoption of the German Kanzler principle[4] (which requires at least a majority – 61 out of the 120 Knesset members – to topple the government). All these important provisions are due to improve the stability and effective functioning of the government.

An indicator to this effect is an opinion poll conducted by the Israeli Gallop group for *Ma'ariv* (an Israeli evening newspaper).[5] The respondents were asked the hypothetical question: Provided that the next election will be held by a PR nation-wide single-ballot list system, for what party would you vote?

The results of the poll demonstrate the salutary effects of the newly established parliamentary system in improving the stability of the government, by increasing the representation of the two major parties (Likud and Labor), and reducing the sectorial representation in the Knesset.

As noted in **chapter 5**, the two-ballot system used under the revoked premier–parliamentary system brought about a distinct reduction in the representation of the two major parties and an impressive increase in the representation of the small and medium-sized parties, causing greater fragmentation and fractionalization of the Knesset. Thus the stability and effective functioning of the government was greatly undermined.

According to the results of the *Ma'ariv* poll, the two major parties, Likud and Labor, would significantly improve their representation in the Knesset. The two parties together would attain 70 seats (the Likud 43 seats, and Labor 27), as against 45 seats they posses together in the present Fifteenth Knesset. Thus, in the upcoming Sixteenth Knesset should they wish to join forces they would most probably be able to pass laws, including basic laws, which require a majority of at least 61 members of the Knesset.

No less important is the diminution in the power of the sectorial parties, as predicted by the *Ma'ariv* poll. Thus, for instance, the Religious Parties would attain only 19 seats in the next Knesset as against 27 in the present Fifteenth Knesset; the Arab parties would attain 8 seats instead of the present 10 seats; and the parties representing the Russian Jews, i.e., Yisrael Ba'Aliya and Yisrael Beitenu, would also lose about a third of their representation in the present Fifteenth Knesset.

The right-wing bloc, together with the religious parties, would, as predicted by the *Ma'ariv* poll, receive 66 seats; thus the leader of this bloc (at the present, Prime Minister Sharon) would have no problem in forming a coalition.

Thus, even though other factors than the change in the governmental and electoral systems may influence the results of the elections to the Sixteenth Knesset, the polls indicate that the newly established parliamentary system will increase significantly the chances of forming stable coalitions, and improve the effective functioning of the government.

Notes

Preface

1   D. W. Rae, *The Political Consequences of Electoral Laws* (New Haven and London: Yale University Press, 1967).

2   A. Lijphart, "The Political Consequences of Electoral Laws, 1945–1985", *American Political Science Review*, vol. 84, no. 2, June 1990; A. Lijphart, *Electoral Systems and Party Systems: A Study of Twenty-Seven Democracies* (New York: Oxford University Press, 1994); A. Lijphart (ed.), *Parliamentary Versus Presidential Government* (New York: Oxford University Press, 1992).

Chapter 1   *Main Characteristics of the Electoral System to the Knesset*

1   For a collection and elaborate discussion of the electoral laws, see Zvi Jaffe, *Chukei Habechirot Laknesset* [Laws of election to the Knesset] (Tel Aviv: Am Oved, 1973).

2   D. W. Rae, *The Political Consequences of Electoral Laws* (New Haven and London: Yale University Press, 1967), pp. 19–21.

3   For a detailed discussion of electoral formulas, see E. Lakeman, *How Democracies Vote* (London: Faber and Faber, 1969), chs. 5 and 6, and Rae, *Political Consequences*, pp. 21–39.

4   For data on the first eight Knessets see A. Brichta, *Democracy and Elections* (in Hebrew) (Tel Aviv: Am Oved, 1977), pp. 45–6. For the Ninth Knesset see A. Brichta, "The 1977 Elections and the Future of Electoral Reform in Israel", in H. Penniman (ed.), *Israel at the Polls 1977* (Washington, DC: American Enterprise Institute, 1979), p. 43.

5   A great number of articles have been written on this subject. The discussion of the arguments of the critics and the supporters of the present electoral system is based on the following sources, all in Hebrew:

The arguments of the critics: Abba Eban, "Shinui Mistar Habechirot" [The need to change the electoral system], *Molad*, October 1951, pp. 367–74; Yigal Eilam, "Bechirot U'mishtar Demokrati" [Elections and democracy], *Molad*, June 1962, pp. 175–81; Abraham Weinshel, "Bechirot Yachassiot o' Ezoriyot"

[Proportional representation or a district system], *Ha'uma*, vol. 20, 1969; David Bar-Rav-Hai, "Shinui Shitat Habechirot – Keitzad?" [How to change the electoral system?], *Ott*, vol. 1. no. 2, 1967; and two books, Meir Bareli, *Iyunim B'shitat Bechirot* [The case against proportional representation] (Tel Aviv: Am Oved, 1971), and Gad Yaacobi and Ehud Gera, *Hahofesh Livchor* [The freedom to choose] (Tel Aviv: Am Oved, 1975).

The argument of the supporters: Shlomo Avineri, "Shitat Habechirot Hateuna He Shinui?" [Is there a need to change the present system?], *Molad*, April 1962; Moshe Seliger, "Ideologia Ubechirot" [Ideology and elections], *Molad*, October 1960; Ze-ev Sternhal, "Kvutzot Lachatz Ubechirot Rubiot" [Pressure groups and plurality systems], *Ovnaim*, vol. 2, 1962; Joseph Shofman, "Democratia Bemivcahn Bechirot" [The challenge of democratic elections], *Ha'uma*, June 1963.

6   B. Akzin, "The Role of Parties in Israeli Democracy", *Journal of Politics*, vol. 17, November 1955, p. 508.

7   G. Sartori, "Representational Systems", *International Encyclopedia of Social Sciences*, vol. 13 (New York: Macmillan, 1968), p. 466.

8   G. Sartori, "European Political Parties: The Case of Polarized Pluralism", in Joseph LaPalombara and Myron Weiner (eds.), *Political Parties and Political Development* (Princeton University Press, 1966), p. 160.

Chapter 2 *The Struggle for Electoral Reform*

1   Moetzet Hamedina Hazmanit (Provisional State Council), Protocol, 28 October 1948, pp. 26–32.

2   For an account of Ben-Gurion's efforts to change the electoral system and for a summary of his position on this issue, see his *Medinat Yisrael HaMehudeshet* (The revived State of Israel) (Tel Aviv: Am Oved, 1969), pp. 575–9.

3   The Center met on 16 September 1954 and, according to Ben-Gurion, approved the proposal for adopting a simple-majority constituency system by a vote of 52 to 6; *ibid.*, p. 578.

4   "Hatsaat Chok Mishal-am al Shitat Ha-Behirot la-Knesset – 1958" [A Bill for a Referendum on the Electoral System for the Fourth Knesset, 1958] (tabled by MK Y. Almogi), *Divrei ha-Knesset* [Knesset Records] 25, pp. 531–3; and "Hatsaat Chok Mishal-am al Shitat Ha-Behirot la-Knesset Ha-Reviit, 1958" (tabled by MK Y. Serlin), *Divrei ha-Knesset* [Knesset Records] 25, pp. 533–5.

5   *Ibid.*, p. 517.

6   *Ibid.*, This motion was approved by a vote of 58 to 53.

7   "Hatsaat Chok Yesod: Ha-Knesset (Tikun Mispar 3)", [Basic Law: The Knesset (Amendment no. 3)], *Divrei ha-Knesset* [Knesset Records] 27, p. 2962.

8   G. Yaacobi and E. Gera, *Hahofesh Livhor* [Freedom to choose] (Tel Aviv: Am Oved, 1975), p. 59.

9   *Ibid.*, p. 58–106.

10 See *Divrei ha-Knesset* [Knesset Records], session 36 of the Eighth Knesset, pp. 737–51.
11 Basic Law: The Knesset (Amendment), 1977, draft proposal by the Alignment and the Likud in the Eighth Knesset.
12 The debate on the proposal in the Constitution Law and Justice Committee began in March 1977. The Eighth Knesset dissolved in April 1977.
13 The principles of the coalition agreement were published in *Ma'ariv*, 25 October 1977.
14 S. Sager, *The Parliamentary System of Israel* (Syracuse, NY: Syracuse University Press: 1985), p. 50.
15 For the 1965 figures see Yaacobi and Gera, *Hahofesh Livhor* [Freedom to choose], p. 55. For the 1987 figures see B. Zusser (ed.), *The Political System of Israel* (Hebrew), provisional edition (Tel Aviv: Bar Ilan University, 1987), p. 490.
16 It was referred by the Constitution Law and Justice Committee for the first reading on 17 March 1987.
17 *Hatsaat Choka L'Medinat Israel* [A proposed constitution for the State of Israel] (np, nd), p. 16.
18 See A. Lijphart, "The Demise of the Last Westminster System? Comments on the Report of New Zealand's Royal Commission on the Electoral System", *Electoral Studies*, vol. 6, 1987, pp. 97–103; J. Eckhard, "Split Voting in the Federal Republic of Germany: An Analysis of the Federal Elections from 1953–1987", *Electoral Studies*, vol. 7, 1987, pp. 109–24; J. Eckhard, "The West German Electoral System: The Case for Reform, 1949–1987", *West European Politics*, vol. 10, 1987, pp. 434–48; R. Taagepera and M. S. Shugart, *Seats and Votes: The Effects and Determinants of Electoral Systems* (New Haven and London: Yale University Press, 1989), pp. 230–2.

Chapter 3   *Proposed Electoral Reforms for the Elections to the Knesset*

1 F. A. Hermens, *Europe between Democracy and Anarchy* (Notre Dame, IN: Notre Dame University Press, 1951), pp. 45–98.
2 G. Van den Berg, *Shitot ha-behirot ba-olam* [Unity among diversity] (Jerusalem: Reuben Mas, 1959), p. 22.
3 E. Lakeman and J. D. Lambert, *Voting in Democracies* (London: Faber & Faber, 1955); J. F. Rose, *Elections and Electors* (London: Eyre and Spottiswood, 1955); A. Dami, "In Support of Proportional Representation", *International Social Science Bulletin*, vol. 3, no. 2, 1951; J. Dreijmanis, "Proportional Representation and Its Effects: The Austrian Experience" *Parliamentary Affairs*, vol. 24, no. 1, Winter 1970/71; H. Eckstein, "The Impact of Electoral Systems on Representative Government", in H. Eckstein and D. Apter (eds), *Comparative Politics* (New York: Macmillan, 1963), pp. 247–54.

4   S. Rokkan, "Electoral Systems", in *The International Encyclopedia of Social Sciences* (Macmillan and Free Press, 1968), p. 19. G. Pomper, too, regards the American two-party system to be rooted in the country's political culture. Thus he remarks: "This tendency has been reinforced by the manner in which the president of the United States is elected. The fact that the nation's chief executive is elected by voters in all the states of the Union allows for only the candidates of parties which are organized on a federal basis to obtain a sufficient number of votes in order to be elected to office." Pomper remarks in this connection: "The Presidency and the electoral system have tended to make unity *desirable* for American parties, and the *social conditions* of the United States have made it possible (my emphasis)." When the national consensus broke down in America in the nineteenth century so did the two-party system, and the country's electoral system was unable to save the Union from civil war. See G. M. Pomper, *Elections in America* (New York: Dodd, Mead & Co., 1971), pp. 49–50.

5   D. W. Rae, *The Political Consequences of Electoral Laws* (New Haven and London: Yale University Press, 1967).

6   A. Lijphart, "The Political Consequences of Electoral Laws, 1945–1985", *American Political Science Review*, vol. 84, no. 2, June 1990; and A. Lijphart, *Electoral Systems and Party Systems: A study of Twenty-Seven Democracies, 1945–1990* (New York: Oxford University Press, 1994).

7   V. Bogdanor, *What is Proportional Representation?* (Oxford: Martin and Robertson, 1984), p. 6.

8   *Ibid.*, p. 7.

9   Our data for all the Knessets are derived from the following sources: *Totsot ha-behirot la-Knesset ha-Shviit u-la-reshuyot ha-mekomiyor* [Election returns for the Seventh Knesset and Local Councils] (Jerusalem: Central Bureau of Statistics, Special Issue no. 461, 1974). *Election Returns for the Ninth Knesset* (in Hebrew) (Jerusalem: Central Bureau of Statistics, Special Issue no. 553, 1978); *Election Returns for the Tenth Knesset* (in Hebrew) (Jerusalem: Central Bureau of Statistics, Special Issue no. 680, 1981); *Election Returns for the Eleventh Knesset* (in Hebrew) (Jerusalem: Central Bureau of Statistics, Special Issue no. 775, 1985); *Election Returns for the Twelfth Knesset* (in Hebrew) (Jerusalem: Central Bureau of Statistics, Special Issue no. 855–6, 1989); *Election Returns for the Thirteenth Knesset* (in Hebrew) (Jerusalem: Central Bureau of Statistics, Special Issue no. 925–6, 1993); *Results of the Elections to the Fourteenth Knesset* (in Hebrew) (Jerusalem: Central Bureau of Statistics, Special Issue no. 1054, 1996); *Statistical Abstract of Israel*, no. 49 (Jerusalem: Central Bureau of Statistics, 1998). The 1999 election results are derived from data supplied by the Central Election Committee, the Knesset, Jerusalem.

10   Rae, *The Political Consequences of Electoral Laws*, p. 75.

11   For an account of Ben-Gurion's efforts to change the electoral system and for a summary of his position on this same issue, see his *Medinat Yisrael Ha-Mehudeshet* [The revived State of Israel] (Tel Aviv: Am Oved, 1969), pp. 575–9.

12   The Center met on 16 Sept. 1954 and, according to Ben-Gurion, approved the proposal for adopting a simple-majority constituency system by a vote of 52 to 6; *ibid.*, p. 578. According to *Zmanim* (Hebrew Daily), 9 Sepember 1954, p. 1, the precise count was 52 in favor, 6 opposed, and 17 abstentions.

13   Z. Vilnai, *Atlas 1968: Shnat esrim li-medinat Yisrael* [Atlas 1968: Twenty years of the State of Israel] (Jerusalem: Jerusalem University Press, 1968), p. 31, maps 28–9.

14   Differences in the size of electoral districts are apparently unavoidable under the simple-majority constituency system in Britain; see Lakeman and Lambert, *Voting in Democracies*, p. 57. According to Lakeman, even after the constituencies reform in 1950 there were 39,261 voters in the smallest electoral district, and 80,568 in the largest. The average for constituencies was 55,000 voters. Nor were the distortions in representation done away with before the February 1974 elections. Following the reform, there were 25,007 voters in the smallest electoral district and 96,380 in the largest, making for a distribution of representation in a ratio of 3.8:1. Furthermore, 10 percent of the constituencies in 1974 had less than 50,000 voters. Dissatisfaction with the representational distortions resulting from the present apportionment of constituencies in Britain has led some scholars to conclude that multi-candidate electoral districts should be established and greater attention given to the distortions created by the present system. See P. and M. Bromhead, "Male Representation of the People: 1974 Model", *Parliamentary Affairs*, no. 1, Winter 1976, pp. 17–27.

15   These findings regarding the projected results under a simple-majority system are in accord with the findings of a study examining election results obtained under the same system in the Jerusalem District on the basis of the returns in the elections for the Fourth Knesset. According to this study: "If we were now to attempt to estimate the possible results based on a plurality system in a national election, we should easily conclude that *even if the constituencies were apportioned in an objective manner*, and without prejudice, Greater Mapai (i.e., with Ahdut Avodah) would receive an absolute majority that might come to *more than 100* of the 120 seats (my emphsis)." See B. Liberman, "Shitat behirot rubiyot – le maaseh" [The plurality electoral system – as it really is], *Molad*, July 1965.

16   Rae, *The Political Consequences of Electoral Laws*, pp. 151–2.

17   Rae, *The Political Consequences of Electoral Laws*, p. 27.

18   Rae, *The Political Consequences of Electoral Laws*, p. 152.

19   For British electoral returns, see E. Lakeman, *How Democracies Vote* (London: Faber & Faber, 1970), p. 40.

20   Wolfsohn arrives at similar figures on the basis of returns in the Sixth Knesset elections. According to Wolfsohn's calculations Labor would have returned 79 MKs, whereas Gahal, the religious parties, and the Independent Liberals would together have accounted for 36 MKs. See A. Wolfsohn, *Behirot azoriyot bi-Medinat Yisrael* [Constituency elections in the State of Israel] (Haifa:

Halevanon, 1968), pp. 76–88. The similarity between my results and those of Wolfsohn and Liberman is evidence that my proposed apportionment of electoral districts is not arbitrary.

21 M. Duverger, *Political Parties* (London: Methuen, 1954), p. 228.

22 For an account of the efforts to prevent the imposition of a 10 percent electoral quota, see *Zmanim* (Hebrew Daily), 13 December 1953 and 22 December 1953.

23 The Mapai Knesset faction consisted of 45 MKs, and that of the General Zionists, of 20 MKs. Between them they could therefore have obtained an absolute majority of 65 votes.

24 On Mapai's motives for withdrawing from the proposal, see *Zmanim*, 16 August 1954, p. 1; and "Keitsad nesheneh et shitat ha-behirot" [How are we to change the electoral system], *Ovnaiim*, vol. 5, 1965, p. 45.

25 Rae, *The Political Consequences of Electoral Laws*, p. 113.

26 The effective threshold according to Lijphart is the mean of the upper threshold – $100\%/(M+1)$ – and the lower threshold – $100\%/2M$ – or:

$$T\text{eff} = \frac{50\%}{(M+1)} + \frac{50\%}{2M}$$

see A. Lijphart, *Electoral Systems and Party Systems*, p. 27.

27 "Hatsaat hok mishal-am al shitat ha-behirot la-Knesset ha-reviit, 1958" [A bill for a referendum on the electoral system for the Fourth Knesset, 1958] (tabled by MK Y. Serlin), *Divrei ha-Knesset* [Knesset Records], vol. 25, pp. 533–5; see also debate, pp. 479–82.

28 D. Bar-Rav-Hai, "Le-birur shitat ha-behirot la-Knesset" [A consideration of the system of Elections for the Knesset], *Ha-poel ha-tsair*, June 1969. Since the report of the Dov Yosef Committee is unpublished to date, I have had to rely on the discussion of the proposal contained in the article by Mr. Bar-Rav-Hai, who was a member of the committee. Findings concerning a number of proposals for electoral reform in Israel have been published by Gad Yaakobi and Ehud Gera, *Hahofesh Livhor* [Freedom to choose] (Tel Aviv: Am Oved, 1975), p. 65).

29 "Hatsaat hok mishal-am", pp. 533–4.

30 Rae, *The Political Consequences of Electoral Laws*, p. 21.

31 Rae, *The Political Consequences of Electoral Laws*, p. 119.

32 Rae, *The Political Consequences of Electoral Laws*, p. 124.

33 A comparison of our findings with those of the Dov Yosef Committee shows, once again, that our apportionment of electoral districts is not arbitrary. The comparison carried out in regard to returns in the elections to the Sixth and Seventh Knessets was done in order to assess the theoretical effect of the size of electoral districts and the formula of seat apportionment on the results of elections in three-member constituencies.

34 D. Bar-Rav-Hai, "*Shinui shitat ha-behirot–Keitsad?*" [Changing the electoral system–How should it be done?], *Ot*, no. 2, 1967.

35 See the effects of the d'Hondt formula on the proportionality of the results in A. Lijphart, *Electoral Systems and Party Systems*, p. 96.

36 Rae, *The Political Consequences of Electoral Laws*, p. 31.
37 This district comprises the following settlements: the municipality of Herzliyah, Bnei Brak, and Ramat Gan; the local councils of Kfar Shemaryahu and Ramat ha-Sharon; the district councils of ha-Yarkon, Ono and Mifalot Afek.
38 This district includes the municipality of Tel Aviv–Jaffa.
39 This district consists of the following settlements: the municipalities of Givatayim, Bat Yam, and Hulon; the local councils of Kiryat Ono, Azur, and Or Yehudah; the district council of Modiin.
40 Lakeman, *Voting in Democracies*, Appendix LI. For detailed data on district magnitude see especially A. Lijphart, *Electoral Systems and Party Systems*, ch. 2, tables 2.1–2.8.
41 Rae, *The Political Consequences of Electoral Laws*, pp. 42–4, table 2.1.
42 According to Rae, the determining factor is not the number of districts but the average magnitude of districts – i.e., the number of elected representatives. Hence in 15 districts of relatively small magnitude as regards the average number of representatives per constituency, the country's big parties would increase their advantage as a result of the division of the Tel Aviv subdistrict.
43 Rae, *The Political Consequences of Electoral Laws*, Differentiaton Proposition Twelve, p. 153.
44 Rae, *The Political Consequences of Electoral Laws*, p. 39.
45 Rae, *The Political Consequences of Electoral Laws*, pp. 38–9.
46 The proposal is included in the Appendix of Yaakobi and Gera, *Hahofesh Livhor* [Freedom to choose], pp. 212–21.
47 According to the Yaakobi proposal, the formula determining the nation-wide quota would be: total valid ballots divided by 30; see "Yaakobi Proposal", sec. 8, par. 21 (c) 1. On the basis of Gad Yaakobi's proposal, the nation-wide quota in the Seventh Knesset elections would have been: 1,367,743 total valid ballots minus 127,058 (the valid votes cast for the party lists that failed to meet Yaakobi's minimum electoral quota of 3 percent). The nation-wide quota for the Seventh Knesset was 46,356. The data for the results of the Seventh Knesset elections are from *Totsot ha-behirot la-Knesset ha-Shviit u-la-rashuyot ha-mekomiyot* (see note 9 in this chapter).
48 This proposition is in line with the two basic rules which specify that district size and the formula of apportionment of seats are the two major factors determining election results. The smaller the electoral districts in terms of number of elected representatives, the greater the advantage of strong parties. See Rae, *The Political Consequences of Electoral Laws*, esp. pp. 15–154. Indeed, Yaakobi proposes that district magnitude be reduced by abandoning the present system of treating the country as a single constituency with 120 representatives, for a system in which there would be 18 five-member districts plus a nation-wide constituency with 30 representatives. On the other hand, the formula for distributing seats gives an obvious advantage to the two biggest parties by setting a high minimum electoral quota of 3 percent nationally.

49 "*Hatsaat hok pratit le-shinui shitat ha-behirot la-Knesset*" [A private member's bill for changing the system of elections to the Knesset] (tabled by MK Boaz Moab). From a copy of the bill privately duplicated by Mr. Moab on a hectograph.

50 See A. Lijphart, "The Political Consequences of Electoral Laws, 1945–1985", *American Political Science Review*, June 1990.

51 Rae, *The Political Consequences of Electoral Laws*, p. 84.

52 Rae, *The Political Consequences of Electoral Laws*, p. 74.

53 Rae, *The Political Consequences of Electoral Laws*, p. 76.

54 See G. Sartori, "Political Development and Political Engineering", in J. D. Montgomery and A. O. Hirschman (eds.), *Public Policy*, vol. 17 (Cambridge, MA: Harvard University Press, 1968).

55 See S. P. Huntington, "One Soul at a Time: Political Science and Political Reform", *American Political Science Review*, vol. 82, no. 1, March 1988, pp. 3–10.

Chapter 4   *The New Premier–Parliamentary System in Israel*

1 G. Sartori, "Neither Presidentialism nor Parliamentarism", in J. Linz and A. Valenzuela (eds.), *The Failure of Presidential Democracy* (Baltimore, MD: Johns Hopkins University Press, 1994), p. 115.

2 A. Ljjphart (ed.), *Parliamentary Versus Presidential Government* (New York: Oxford University Press, 1992), p. 1.

3 Sartori, "Neither Presidentialism nor Parliamentarism", p. 109.

4 *Ibid.*, p. 106.

5 See J. Blondel, "Party Systems and Patterns of Government in Western Democracies", *Canadian Journal of Political Science*, vol. I, 1968, pp. 180–200. My calculation is based on the index developed by Blondel. According to this index, the calculation of the average duration of western governments is based on an operational definition of a government using two criteria: (1) that the government served under the same prime minister, and (2) that the government was supported by the same party or parties in the parliament.

6 D. Korn, *Time in Gray* (in Hebrew) (Tel Aviv: Zmora-Bitan, 1994), ch. 15.

7 L. Diamond and E. Sprinzak (eds.), *Israeli Democracy Under Stress* (Boulder, CO: Liynne Rienner, 1993), pp. 3–4 and p. 362 (emphasis added).

8 For the 1965 figures, see Gad Yaacobi and Ehud Gera, *Hahofesh Livhor* [Freedom to choose] (Tel Aviv: Am Oved, 1975), p. 55, n. 11. For the 1987 figures, see B. Zusser (ed.), *The Political System of Israel* (in Hebrew) (Tel Aviv: Bar Ilan University, 1987), p. 490 of the provisional edition.

9 See chapter 3.

10 For a detailed description of the saga of this law, see G. Allon, *Direct Election* (in Hebrew) (Tel Aviv: Bitan, 1995); G. Bechor, *Constitution for Israel* (in Hebrew) (Or-Yehuda: Maariv, 1996).

11 For the figures, see R. Hazan, "Presidential Parliamentarism", *Electoral Studies*, vol. 15, 1996, pp. 24–8.
12 G. Doron, "The Political Rationale of Electoral Reforms in Democratic Systems", in G. Doron (ed.), *The Electoral Revolution* (in Hebrew) (Tel Aviv: Hakibbutz Hameuchad, 1996), p. 73.
13 Basic Law: The Government, *Sefer Hachukim*, 1396, 14 April 1992, p. 214.
14 Amendment no. 9 of the Basic Law: The Government, passed by the Knesset on 18 December 2000, *Sefer Hachukim*, 1762, p. 48.
15 Basic Law: The Knesset, amendment no. 10, passed by the Knesset, 1 August 1999, *Sefer Hachukim,* 1772, p. 258.
16 Sartori, "Neither Presidentialism nor Parliamentarism", p. 106.
17 A. Arian, "The Israeli Election for Prime Minister and the Knesset 1996", *Electoral Studies*, vol. 17, 1996, p. 574.
18 S. Mainwaring, "Presidentialism in Latin America", *Latin American Research*, vol. 25, 1990.
19 Sartori, "Neither Presidentialism nor Parliamentarism", p. 107; F. W. Riggs, "The Survival of Presidentialism in America: Para-constitutional Practices", *International Political Science Review*, vol. 9, no. 4, 1988, pp. 247–78.
20 G. Bingham Powell, Jr., "Contemporary Democracies: Participation, Stability and Violence", in A. Lijphart (ed.), *Parliamentary Versus Presidential Government*; A. T. Bayliss, "Governing by Committee: Collegial Leadership in Advanced Societies", in A. Lijphart (ed.), *Parliamentary Versus Presidential Government*, pp. 223–43.
21 Sartori, "Neither Presidentialism nor Parliamentarism", p. 110.

Chapter 5   *The Knesset as a Representative Assembly*

1 H. Eulau, "Changing Views of Representation", in I. De Sola Pool (ed.), *Contemporary Political Science* (New York, 1967), p. 54.
This leads Birch to the conclusion that there is not a single meaning of the term, but that there are four different types of representation "which can be appropriately described as symbolic representation, delegated representation, microcosmic representation and elective representation". A. H. Birch, *Representation* (London, 1972), p. 24.
2 H. Pitkin, *The Concept of Representation* (Berkeley, 1967), p. 9.
3 F. Mosher, *Democracy and the Public Service* (New York, 1968), p. 11.
4 *Ibid.*, pp. 11–12.
5 Eulau, "Changing Views of Representation", p. 54.
6 Mosher, *Democracy and the Public Service*, p. 13.
7 S. Krislov, *The Negro in Federal Employment* (Minneapolis: Minnesota University Press, 1967), ch. 3.
8 G. Sartori, "Representational Systems", in the *International Encyclopedia of Social Sciences*, vol. 13 (New York: Macmillan, 1968), p. 466.

9 Birch, *Representation*, p. 20, emphasis added.
10 H. Herzog, et al., *The Israeli Politician: A Social and Political Profile of Activists in Party Centers of Labor and Herut* (Jerusalem: Jerusalem Institute for the Research of Israel, 1989) (in Hebrew).
11 A. Arian, "Incumbency in Israel's Knesset", in A. Somit, et al. (eds.), *The Victorious Incumbent: A Threat to Democracy?* (Aldershot: Dartmouth, 1996), pp. 71–102.

Chapter 6 *Proposals for Presidential Government in Israel*

1 As a result of the great disillusionment with the new premier–parliamentary system there are some thoughts of reverting to the idea of adopting a presidential system. For instance, prime minister Barak is favorably considering the adoption of the presidential system. In this case he is joining a number of politicians who were in favor of the presidential system, such as the former PM Itzhak Rabin, and the former minister of justice Shmuel Tamir. However, the whole subject was not given the same theoretical and practical consideration as the case of electoral reform. For the pronouncement of PM Barak, see *Haaretz*, 29 November 2000.
2 We prefer the term "quasi-presidential", when referring to the Fifth French Republic, to that of "semi-presidential", suggested by Maurice Duverger, because his classification of semi-presidential systems includes in the same category strong presidential systems, such as that of France, and weak figurehead presidential systems, such as those of Iceland and Austria. Moreover, from the standpoint of stability and effectiveness, the French presidential system provides for both a stable and an effective Executive, while the Finnish semi-presidential system for instance, according to Durverger himself, could not provide the country with stable government. Thus, in sixty years, sixty cabinets have succeeded each other in Finland. See Maurice Duverger, "A New Political System Model: Semi-Presidential Government", *European Journal of Political Research*, vol. 8, March 1980, pp. 165–87, esp. figure 1 on p. 179 and p. 183.
3 B. B. Schaffer, "The Concept of Preparation: Some Questions About the Transfer of Systems of Government", *World Politics*, vol. 18, October 1965; and B. Munslow, "Why Has the Westminster Model Failed in Africa?" *Parliamentary Affairs*, vol. 36, Spring 1983.
4 See William J. Crotty, *Political Reform and the American Experiment* (New York: Crowell, 1977), p. 267.
5 H. J. Laski, "The Parliamentary and Presidential Systems", *Public Administration Review*, vol. 4, Autumn 1944.
6 See chapter 5.
7 G. Rahat, *The Politics of Reform of the Israeli Regime Structure*, unpublished Ph.D. dissertation, Jerusalem: Hebrew University, 2000 (in Hebrew).
8 See J. Blondel, "Party Systems and Patterns of Government in Western

Democracies", *Canadian Journal of Political Science*, vol. I, 1968, pp. 180–200. Our calculation is based on the index developed by Blondel. According to this index, the calculation of the average duration of western governments is based on an operational definition of a government using two criteria: 1. The government served under the same prime minister. 2. The government was supported by the same party or parties in the parliament. For similar definitions of stability see L. C. Dodd, *Coalitions and Parliamentary Government* (Princeton NJ: Princeton University Press, 1976), p. 122; and also G. Bingham Powell, *Contemporary Democracies* (Cambridge, MA: Harvard University Press, 1982), p. 18. There are slight differences in the definitions of stability among the authors. Dodd defines the duration of a cabinet "So long as there is no change in the parties that compose the cabinet." Powell has a slightly more rigorous definition. In his view "A parliamentary government is here defined as 'enduring' as long as it has the same composition of political parties holding cabinet positions and the individual prime minister has not been forced from office involuntarily." We prefer Blondel's definition as being more comprehensive. Thus for instance in the Israeli case, although Ben-Gurion was not forced from office involuntarily in 1953, his departure and replacement by Moshe Sharett brought about a significant change in the policies of the new cabinet.

9   Calculated on the basis of Gad Yaacobi, *The Government* (in Hebrew), second edition (Tel Aviv: Am Oved, 1980), Appendix, pp. 338–57. We would like to point out that, contrary to Dodd's findings, oversized coalitions in Israel are much more durable than minimum winning coalitions. The average duration of an oversized coalition between 1949 and 1977 was 19.2 months, while the average duration of a minimum winning coalition was only 8.4 months. Dodd's exclusion of Israel from his comprehensive study on the basis that a country in a continuous state of war is particularly suited for the formation of oversized coalitions, defies the facts: firstly, because as Felsenthal demonstrates, more than half of Israel's coalitions were minimum winning, and secondly, because the duration of most of the coalitions and subsequently their termination of office was very seldom due to circumstances related to Israel's security. For Dodd's argument see Dodd, *Coalitions and Parliamentary Government*, p. 23n. For Felsenthal's findings see D. S. Felsenthal, "Aspects of Coalition Payoffs: The Case of Israel", *Comparative Political Studies*, vol. 19, July 1979, p. 154. The calculation of the duration of oversized and minimum winning coalitions is based on pp. 155–6, table I. For a classification of the causes for cabinets' termination of office, see A. Brichta, *Democracy and Elections* (in Hebrew) (Tel Aviv: Am Oved, 1977), pp. 50–2.

10 The "status quo" agreement is included in a letter sent by Ben-Gurion to the leader of Agudat Yisrael, Rabbi Maimon in 1947, expressing the willingness of the secular parties to respect the demands of the Orthodox groups with regard to Personal Status Law, the Shabbat, education and Kashrut (dietary

laws). The letter is reproduced in D. Shimshoni, *Israeli Democracy* (New York: Free Press, 1982), p. 478.

11 Israel "Law and Administrative Ordinance 5708 – 1948", *Laws of Israel* (Jerusalem: Government Printer, 1948), p. 7.

12 Felsenthal, "Aspects of Coalition Payoffs: The Case of Israel", p. 163.

13 R. Rose: "Conclusion", in R. Rose and E. Suleiman (eds.), *Presidents and Prime Ministers* (Washingon DC: American Enterprise Institute, 1980), p. 288.

14 R. Shogan, *None of the Above: Why Presidents Fail and What Can Be Done About It* (New York and Scarborough, Ontario: New American Library, 1982), p. 13.

15 F. Greenstein, "Change and Continuity in the Modern Presidency", in A. King (ed.), *The New American Political System* (Washington DC: American Enterprise Institute, 1978), p. 75.

16 R. E. Neustadt, *Presidential Power*, revised edn. (New York: Wiley, 1980).

17 Greenstein, "Change and Continuity in the Modern Presidency", p. 83.

18 Articles 8, 10, 11, 12, 16 and 39 of the Constitution of the Fifth Republic. See especially articles 38 and 48 for the broad powers of the prime minister, and the cabinet, in the process of legislation.

19 The State of Emergency was declared on 21 May 1948 and has never been rescinded. For the declaration, see *Official Gazette* no. 2, 21 May 1948.

20 M. Debré, quoted in S. Berger, *The French Political System* (New York: Random House, 1974), p. 38.

21 *Ibid.*

22 V. Bogdanor, "Conclusion: Electoral Systems and Party Systems", in V. Bogdanor and D. Butler (eds.), *Democracy and Elections: Electoral Systems and their Consequences* (Cambridge: Cambridge University Press, 1983), p. 252.

23 G. Bechor, *Constitution for Israel* (in Hebrew) (Or-Yehuda: Maariv. 1996).

24 D. Goldey and P. Williams, "France", in V. Bogdanor and D. Butler (eds.), *Democracy and Elections: Electoral Systems and their Consequences* (Cambridge: Cambridge University Press, 1983), p. 81, and also J. R. Frears, *France in the Giscard Presidency* (London: Allen and Unwin, 1981), pp. 69–74.

25 Goldey and Williams, "France", p. 82.

26 See Avraham Brichta, "The 1977 Elections and the Future of Electoral Reform in Israel", in H. Penniman (ed.), *Israel at the Polls 1977*, (Washington DC: American Enterprise Institute, 1979), pp. 30–50, and chapters 2 and 3 in this book.

27 On the pervasiveness of politics in Israeli society see especially Benjamin Akzin, "The Role of Parties in Israeli Democracy", *Journal of Politics*, vol. 17, November 1955, pp. 507–45. For a more recent statement see D. Horowitz, "More than a Change in Government", *The Jerusalem Quarterly,* vol. 5, Fall 1977, esp. pp. 18–19.

28 F. C. Engelmann, "Austria: The Pooling of Opposition", in R. A. Dahl (ed.),

Political Oppositions in Western Democracies (New York: Yale University Press, 1966), p. 267 (emphasis added).
29   Goldey and Williams, "France", p. 74.

Chapter 7   The Political Consequences of the Direct Elections of the Prime Minister and the Heads of Local Councils: A Comparison between Local and National Levels

1   See "The Law of Local Authorities (The Election of the Head of the Local Authority and his Deputies and Term of Office)", 1975, *Sefer Hachukim*, 5735, p. 211, *Sefer Hachukim*, 5736, p. 151.
2   In the elections to the local councils the number of candidates elected on a list is defined by a quota. The quota is the number derived by dividing the total number of valid votes by the number of candidates elected to the council. The threshold in the elections to the local councils is 75 percent of the quota.
3   A. Hect, *Adversary Council in the Local Government* (Jerusalem: The Jerusalem Center for Public Policy, August 1993).
4   A. Brichta, "Do not shed a Tear: The Decline of Parties in the Local Government", in D. Korn (ed.), *The Demise of Parties in Israel* (Tel Aviv: Ha'Kibutz Ha'Meohad, 1998), pp. 263–73 (Hebrew).
5   Hect, *Adversary Council in the Local Government.*

Concluding Remarks: Toward Electoral Reform

1   G. Sartori, "The Party-Effects of Electoral Systems", in R. Hazan, and M. Maor, "Parties, Elections and Cleavages: Israel in Comparative and Theoretical Perspective", Special Issue of *Israel Affairs,* vol. 6, no. 2, Winter 1999, p. 13.
2   D. Horowitz, and M. Lisak, *The Origins of the Israeli Polity: The Political System of the Jewish Community in Palestine Under the Mandate* (Tel Aviv: Am Oved, 1977).
3   L. Guttman, "Whither Israel's Political Parties?" *Jewish Frontier*, vol. 28, no. 11, December 1961.
4   G. Rahat, "The Politics of Reform in Israel: How the Israeli Mixed System Came to Be", in M. S. Shugart and M. P. Wattenberg (eds.), *Mixed-Member Electoral Systems: The Best of Both Worlds? (*Oxford University Press, forthcoming).
5   Sartori, "The Party-Effects of Electoral Systems", p. 27.
6   A. Lijphart, *Electoral Systems and Party Systems: A Study of Twenty-Seven Democracies, 1945–1990* (New York: Oxford University Press, 1994), p. 139.
7   *Ibid.*, p. 151.

Postscript

1 See *Basic Law: The Government*, accepted by the Knesset on 7 March 2001.
2 *Ibid.*, paragraph 46.
3 *Ibid.*, paragraphs 7–10.
4 *Ibid.*, paragraph 28.
5 See *Ma'ariv*, 16 March 2001.

Glossary

Agudat Yisrael / Israel (also Aguda)   Ultra-Orthodox Ashkenazi religious political party with non-Zionist ideology. Has been in the opposition from 1952 to 1977, and since then has been in many of the coalitions, though not in ministerial positions.

Agudat Yisrael Workers Party   This party holds somewhat more moderate views on religious matters than does Agudat Yisrael, and tends to reflect a more left-wing stance in social and economic spheres.

Ahdut Haavoda   (a) Political organization founded in 1919 and dominant in the politics of the Yishuv (pre-state Jewish settlement); (b) left-wing party that joined Mapai and Rafi in 1968 to form the Israel Labor Party.

Alignment   (a) Name of election list in 1965 composed of Mapai and Ahdut Haavoda; (b) name of election list between 1969 and 1984 composed of Labor and Mapam.

Ashkenazim   Jews whose origin is generally the countries of Europe. Arising from a Hebrew word meaning "German" it has taken on a broader definition that includes not only German Jews but those of Eastern and Central Europe and Russia as well.

Bader–Ofer Amendment   Law that sets the method of distributing the last seats to be allocated in the Knesset election. The allocation of seats by this formula is in principle similar to that of d'Hondt.

Balad   Radical, anti-Zionist Arab party headed by Azmi Bashara. Calling for the establishment of "One State for Two Peoples".

Basic Law   Legislation of constitutional stature. Collection of Basic Laws to form the Israeli constitution.

Glossary

Black Panthers   A protest movement in the early 1970s comprised mostly of oriental Jews demanding greater equality and social justice for Jews of Sephardic origin.

Citizens' Rights Movement (CRM)   Left-wing party now part of Meretz.

Council of the Tora Sages   Committees of rabbis of Ultra-Orthodox parties (Agudat Israel, Degel Hatorah and Shas) that provide political and religious decisions for those parties.

Degel Hatora   Ultra-Orthodox non-Zionist party, which split from Agudat Israel.

Democratic Front for Peace and Equality (DFPE)   Arab communist and nationalist list, dominated by Rakah.

Democratic Movement for Change (DMC)   Center party headed by Yigael Yadin; ran only in 1977 and won 15 seats.

d'Hondt System   Allocation of seats in parliament taking into consideration the relative strength of the competing lists. According to the d'Hondt formula seats are awarded sequentially to parties having the highest average number of votes per seat until all seats are allocated. The d'Hondt formula uses the integers 1,2,3,4, and so on, in the allocation of seats.

Eretz Israel   Land of Israel, denoting the biblical Promised Land.

Free Center   A splinter group from Herut in 1967, a part of the Likud from 1973 to 1977, and a component of the DMC in 1977. Headed by Shmuel Tamir.

Gahal   Originally, an acronym for Herut–Liberal bloc. Established as a joint list in 1965; expanded in 1973 and called the Likud.

General Zionists   Right-of-center bourgeois party that joined with the Progressives between 1961 and 1965 and was known as the Liberal Party.

Gerrymandering   The apportion, or reapportion of electoral districts in such a way that the party responsible for making the apportionment gains an inequitable number of seats in the legislature. The term originates from a redistricting bill in Massachusetts in 1812, which gave undue advantage to the party of the Governor, Elbridge Gerry, and in which the boundaries of one of the new districts resembled a salamander. Of significance in countries using a non-proportional electoral system.

Glossary

Gesher   List headed by David Levi after leaving the Likud before the 1996 election. Eventually formed a joint list with Likud and Tzomet in the 1996 elections, and with Ehud Barak's Israel One list before the 1999 elections.

Gush Emunim   Settlement movement, largely religious, active in the territories acquired after the 1967 war and firmly opposed to any territorial compromise.

Halacha   Jewish religious law.

Hapoel Hamizrachi   Religious workers' movement and a major component of the National Religious Party.

Hare Formula (quota)   See Largest Remainder.

Haredim (singular haredi)   Ultra-Orthodox non-Zionists. Literally "awe-inspired", fearful of God's majesty.

Herut   A political party with nationalist ideology, and a major component of the Likud.

Histadrut   The General Federation of Labor, formerly a key economic and political force; since 1994 restyled to focus on trade union matters.

Independent Liberal Party   Formerly the Progressive Party. Part of the Liberal Party between 1961 and 1965. In 1984, part of the Alignment.

Israel Ba'aliya   Russian immigrants' party, headed by Natan Sheranski. Won 7 seats in the 1996 elections and joined the Likud government.

Israel Labor Party   See Labor–Mapam Alignment.

Kach   List of the Jewish Defense League founded by Rabbi Meir Kahane. Disqualified from participating in Knesset elections since 1988 because of its racist ideology.

Kalanterism   The exploitation of a political situation to further personal goals, in particular switching support from one party to another, thereby determining the party that will by able to form the governing coalition.

Kibbutz   Communal settlement sharing production and consumption.

Knesset   Israel's parliament, with 120 members.

Glossary

La'am   A political party that developed from the Rafi faction of Mapai; in 1968 it refused to support the Labor Party, then joined the Likud.

Labor Alignment   See Labor–Mapam Alignment.

Labor–Mapam Alignment   List that included the Labor Party and Mapam; 1969–1984.

Labor Party   One of Israel's major political parties. A Socialist party dominant in the pre-state era and during the first three decades of independence. In the 1999 election comprised the major part of Ehud Barak's Israel One list.

Largest Remainder Formula   A method for allocating seats in the parliament, used for allocating the remaining seats after using a quota, according to the size of the remainders. In Israel it was used with the Hare formula or quota system. The Hare quota is arrived at by dividing the total number of valid votes by the number of seats allocated to a district or nation-wide.

Liberal Party   Middle-class party; a member of Gahal and Likud. Formerly the General Zionists.

Likud (Unity)   One of Israel's major parties. Right-of-center party historically opposed to the return of territories taken after the 1967 war.

Majority Systems   A system of election according to which a candidate needs to attain a majority, namely at least 50 percent +1 vote, in order to get elected. If no candidate is elected on the first ballot, a second ballot is held normally after two weeks, in which usually only the two top candidates are allowed to compete, and the winner is elected. Used in France at the local and national levels, and in Israel it was used for the direct election of the prime minister.

Mandate   The British administration of Palestine by a decision of the League of Nations after the First World War, lasting until 1948.

Mapai   Originally, an acronym for Israel Workers' Party. Created in 1930, it was the dominant party in Israel until its merger in 1968 with Ahdut Haavoda and Rafi to form the Israel Labor Party.

Mapam   Originally an acronym for the United Worker's Party. A left-wing socialist–Zionist party, Mapam was part of the Alignment between 1969 and 1984.

Meimad   Moderate pro-Zionist religious party founded by members who left the NRP.

Glossary

Mercaz   Center-oriented liberal party formed mainly by former Likud leading politicians with "hawkish" orientation and some newcomers with "dovish" orientation.

Meretz   Left-wing party formed by Mapam, the Citizens' Rights Movement, and Shinui.

Mizrachi   A major component of the National Religious Party.

Moledet   Party led by Rehavam Ze'evi ("Gandhi"), calling for the voluntary transfer of Arabs from Israel.

Morasha   Religious party established by Rabbi Haim Druckman together with Agudat Yisrael Workers Pary before the 1984 elections. In 1986 Druckman resigned from Morasha and returned to the National Religious Party (NRP).

Moshav   Cooperative settlement in which production (but usually not consumption) is collective.

National Bloc   Extreme right-wing party.

National Religious Party (NRP)   Zionist and Orthodox religious party, active in settlements in the territories.

National Democratic Alliance (NDA)   An Arab party.

Ometz   List headed by Yigal Horowitz, formerly a member of Rafi. Ran for election in 1984. Joined the Labor bloc in 1984, and the Likud bloc in 1986. In 1988 joined the Likud.

One Nation   Party formed by the head of "The New Histadrut" in order to defend the interests of the trade unions.

Panachage   A special feature of the PR list system used in the parliamentary elections in Luxembourg and Switzerland, which gives each voter as many votes as there are seats in the district, and allows him or her to distribute these votes over two or more parties equally or preferentially. In Luxembourg it is used also in the elections to the European Parliament.

Plurality System   Referred to also as a simple-majority single-ballot system, or "first pass the post" or "winner-takes-all". An electoral system according to which a candidate in a single-member constituency who attains a plurality of votes is declared elected. Used in English-speaking countries, such as the United States, Britain, Canada and India.

Glossary

Progressive List for Peace (PLP)   Established in 1984 as a joint Arab–Jewish list supporting the creation of a Palestinian state alongside the State of Israel.

Progressives   Political party originally supported and dominated by German immigrants. In 1961, merged with the General Zionists to form the Liberal Party. This party split in 1965 and the Progressives took the name Independent Liberals. In 1984, became part of the Alignment.

Proportional Representation   A system of voting designed to produce a result which reflects as accurately as possible the proportional support in votes given to a party in terms of seats in the parliament. Proportional representation tends to preserve the division of party groups existing at the time of its introduction, though it doesn't necessarily increase the number of parties represented in the parliament.

Rafi   Party founded by David Ben-Gurion and others who split from Mapai. Ran once in 1965 and won 10 seats. In 1968, most of the activists (excluding Ben-Gurion) returned and formed the Labor Party along with Mapai and Ahdut Haavoda.

Rakah (New Communist List)   Broke off from the Israel Communist Party in 1965, based primarily on Arab support. In 1977, formed the Democratic Front for Peace and Equality as a joint list with the Black Panthers.

Ratz   Left-wing party formed by Shulamit Aloni in the early 1970s. First participated in the Knsset elections in 1973. In 1992 was the major partner in Meretz.

Religious Front   Joint religious list. Ran for Knesset elections in 1949.

Sephardim   Jews of African and Asian origin. Also called Oriental Jews (*Mizrahiyim*). In the strictest sense of the word the Sephardim (plural of Sephardi) are the Jews who came from the Iberian Peninsula. Today however the word Sephardim has taken a much wider meaning and includes Jewish Communities in North Africa, Iraq, Syria, Greece, and Turkey.

Shas   Ultra-Orthodox religious party established in 1984 with special appeal to Sephardim. Split from Agudat Israel.

Shinui (Change)   Centrist party established as a protest movement after the 1973 Yom Kippur war. Part of the Democratic Movement for Change in 1977, and of Meretz in 1992 and 1996.

Single Transferable Vote (STV)   A PR formula enabling the voters also to cast their votes for individual candidates. The allocation of seats is according to the voters' preferences, instead of party lists.

Glossary

State List   A political party made up originally of Rafi members who refused to reunite with Mapai in 1968.

Tehiya   Extreme nationalist party, which claimed Israel's right to the Land of Israel and opposed the peace treaty with Egypt. Last elected in 1988.

Telem   List formed by Moshe Dayan in 1981 after his departure from the Likud government. Rejoined the government after the war in Lebanon. Split in 1984.

The Third Way   Split form the Labor Party after the Oslo agreement and headed by Avigdor Kahalani. Joined the Likud government in 1996 after winning four seats in that election.

Tzomet   Right-wing party established in 1988 by Raphael Eitan, former IDF chief-of-staff, after splitting from Tehiya. In 1996 formed a joint list with Likud and Gesher.

UAL   United Arab List.

United Torah Jewry (Yahadut Hatorah)   Joint list of Ultra-Orthodox non-Zionist parties, Agudat Israel and Degel Hatorah.

Yahad   Moderate center party headed by Ezer Weizman after his split from the Likud in 1984.

Yishuv   Jewish settlement and communal organization in the pre-state period.

Zionist Congress   Governing body of the World Zionist Organization.

Terms of Knessets

Election	Knesset
21 January 1949	I
30 July 1951	II
26 July 1955	III
3 November 1959	IV
15 August 1961	V
2 November 1965	VI
28 October 1969	VII
31 December 1973	VIII
17 May 1977	IX
30 June 1981	X
23 July 1984	XI
1 November 1988	XII
23 June 1992	XIII
29 May 1996	XIV
17 May 1999	XV

Bibliography

Akzin, B. "The Role of Parties in Israeli Democracy". *Journal of Politics*, vol. 17, November 1955.

Arian, A. "The Israeli Election for Prime Minister and the Knesset 1996". *Electoral Studies*, vol. 17, 1996.

—— "Incumbency in Israel's Knesset". In A. Somit, et al. (eds.), *The Victorious Incumbent: A Threat to Democracy?* Aldershot: Dartmouth, 1996, pp. 71–102.

Avineri, S. "Shitat Habechirot Hateuna He Shinui?" [Is there a need to change the present system?]. *Molad*, April 1962.

Bareli, M. *Iyunim B'shitat Bechirot* [The case against proportional representation]. Tel Aviv: Am Oved, 1971.

Bar-Rav-Hai, D. "Le-birur shitat ha-behirot la-Knesset" [A consideration of the system of elections for the Knesset]. *Ha-poel ha-tsair*, June 1969.

—— "Shinui shitat ha-behirot–Keitsad?" ["Changing the electoral system–How should it be done?"]. *Ot*, no. 2, 1967.

Bayliss, A. T. "Governing by Committee: Collegial Leadership in Advanced Societies". In A. Lijphart (ed.), *Parliamentary Versus Presidential Government*. Oxford: Oxford University Press, 1992.

Bechor, G. *Constitution for Israel* (in Hebrew). Or-Yehuda: Maariv, 1996.

Ben-Gurion, D. *Medinat Yisrael HaMehudeshet* [The revived State of Israel]. Tel Aviv: Am Oved, 1969.

Birch, A. H. *Representation*. London, 1972.

Blondel, J. "Party Systems and Patterns of Government in Western Democracies". *Canadian Journal of Political Science*, vol. I, 1968.

Bogdanor, V. "Conclusion: Electoral Systems and Party Systems". In V. Bogdanor and D. Butler (eds.), *Democracy and Elections: Electoral Systems and their Consequences*. Cambridge: Cambridge University Press, 1983.

—— *What is Proportional Representation?* Oxford: Martin and Robertson, 1984.

Brichta, A. "The 1977 Elections and the Future of Electoral Reform in Israel". In H. Penniman (ed.), *Israel at the Polls 1977*. Washington DC: American Enterprise Institute, 1979.

—— "Do not shed a Tear: The Decline of Parties in the Local Government", in D.

Bibliography

Korn (ed.), *The Demise of Parties in Israel*. Tel Aviv: Ha'Kibutz Ha'Meohad, 1998.

—— *Democracy and Elections* (Hebrew). Tel Aviv: Am Oved, 1977.

Bromhead, P. "Male Representation of the People: 1974 Model". *Parliamentary Affairs*, no. 1, Winter 1976.

Crotty, W. J. *Political Reform and the American Experiment*. New York: Crowell, 1977.

Dami, A. "In Support of Proportional Representation". *International Social Science Bulletin*, vol. 3, 1951.

Debré, M. quoted in Berger, S. *The French Political System*. New York: Random House, 1974.

Diamond, L. and Sprinzak, E. (eds.). *Israeli Democracy Under Stress*. Boulder, CO: Liynne Rienner, 1993.

Dodd, C. L. *Coalitions and Parliamentary Government*. Princeton, NJ: Princeton University Press, 1976.

Doron, G. "The Political Rationale of Electoral Reforms in Democratic Systems". In G. Doron, *The Electoral Revolution* (in Hebrew). Tel Aviv: Hakibbutz Hameuchad, 1996.

Dreijmanis, J. "Proportional Representation and Its Effects: The Austrian Experience". *Parliamentary Affairs*, vol. 24, Winter 1970/71.

Duverger, M. *Political Parties*. London: Methuen, 1954.

—— "A New Political System Model: Semi-Presidential Government". *European Journal of Political Research*, vol. 8, March 1980.

Eban, A. "Shinui Mistar Habechirot" [The need to change the electoral system]. *Molad*, October 1951.

Eckhard, J. "Split Voting in the Federal Republic of Germany: An Analysis of the Federal Elections from 1953–1987". *Electoral Studies*, vol. 7, 1987.

—— "The West German Electoral System: The Case for Reform, 1949–1987". *West European Politics*, vol. 10, 1987.

Eckstein, H. "The Impact of Electoral Systems on Representative Government". In H. Eckstein and D. Apter (eds.), *Comparative Politics*. New York: Macmillan, 1963.

Eilam, Y. "Bechirot U'mishtar Demokrati" [Elections and democracy]. *Molad*, June 1962.

Engelmann, C. F. "Austria: The Pooling of Opposition". In R. A. Dahl (ed.), *Political Oppositions in Western Democracies*. New York: Yale University Press, 1966.

Eulau, H. "Changing Views of Representation". In I. De Sola Pool (ed.), *Contemporary Political Science*. New York, 1967.

Felsenthal, S. D. "Aspects of Coalition Payoffs: The Case of Israel". *Comparative Political Studies*, vol. 19, July 1979.

Frears, R. J. *France in the Giscard Presidency*. London: Allen and Unwin, 1981.

Goldey, D. and Williams, P. "France". In V. Bogdanor and D. Butler (eds.),

Bibliography

Democracy and Elections: Electoral Systems and their Consequences. Cambridge: Cambridge University Press, 1983.

Greenstein, F. "Change and Continuity in the Modern Presidency". In Anthony King (ed.), *The New American Political System*. Washington DC: American Enterprise Institute, 1978.

Guttman, L. "Whither Israel's Political Parties?" *Jewish Frontier*, vol. 28, December 1961.

Hazan, R. "Presidential Parliamentarism". *Electoral Studies*, vol. 15, 1996.

Hermens, F. A. *Europe between Democracy and Anarchy*. Notre Dame, IN: Notre Dame University Press, 1951.

Horowitz, D. and Lisak, M. *The Origins of the Israeli Polity: The Political System of the Jewish Community in Palestine Under the Mandate*. Tel Aviv: Am Oved, 1977.

Horowitz, D. "More than a Change in Government". *The Jerusalem Quarterly*, vol. 5, Fall 1977.

Huntington, P. S. "One Soul at a Time: Political Science and Political Reform". *American Political Science Review*, vol. 82, March 1988.

Jaffe, Z. *Chukei Habechirot Laknesset* [Laws of election to the Knesset]. Tel Aviv: Am Oved, 1973.

Korn, D. *Time in Gray* (in Hebrew). Tel Aviv: Zmora-Bitan, 1994.

Krislov, S. *The Negro in Federal Employment*. Minneapolis: Minnesota University Press, 1967.

Lakeman, E. and Lambert, J. D. *Voting in Democracies*. London: Faber & Faber, 1955.

Lakeman, E. *How Democracies Vote*. London: Faber & Faber, 1969.

Laski, J. H. "The Parliamentary and Presidential Systems". *Public Administration Review*, vol. 4, Autumn 1944.

Liberman, B. "Shitat behirot rubiyot–le maaseh" ["The plurality electoral system – as it really is"]. *Molad*, June 1965.

Lijphart, A. "The Demise of the Last Westminster System? Comments on the Report of New Zealand's Royal Commission on the Electoral System". *Electoral Studies*, vol. 6, 1987.

—— *Democracy in Plural Societies*. New Haven and London: Yale University Press, 1977.

—— "The Political Consequences of Electoral Laws, 1945–1985". *American Political Science Review*, vol. 84, June 1990.

—— *Electoral Systems and Party Systems: A study of Twenty-Seven Democracies, 1945–1990*. New York: Oxford University Press, 1994.

—— (ed.). *Parliamentary Versus Presidential Government*. New York: Oxford University Press, 1992.

Mainwaring, S. "Presidentialism in Latin America". *Latin American Research*, vol. 25, 1990.

Mosher, F. *Democracy and the Public Service*. New York, 1968.

Bibliography

Munslow, B. "Why Has the Westminster Model Failed in Africa?" *Parliamentary Affairs*, vol. 36, Spring 1983.

Neustadt, E. R. *Presidential Power* (revised edn.). New York: Wiley, 1980.

Pitkin, H. *The Concept of Representation*. Berkeley, CA, 1967.

Pomper, G. M. *Elections in America*. New York: Dodd, Mead & Co., 1971.

Powell, Bingham G. *Contemporary Democracies*. Cambridge, MA: Harvard University Press, 1982.

Rae, W. D. *The Political Consequences of Electoral Laws*. New Haven and London: Yale University Press, 1967.

Rahat, G. *The Politics of Reform of the Israeli Regime Structure*. Unpublished Ph.D. dissertation, Jerusalem: Hebrew University, 2000 (in Hebrew).

—— "The Politics of Reform in Israel: How the Israeli Mixed System Came to Be". In M. S. Shugart and M. P. Wattenberg (eds.), *Mixed-Member Electoral Systems: The Best of Both Worlds?* Oxford University Press (forthcoming).

Riggs, F. W. "The Survival of Presidentialism in America: Para-constitutional Practices". *International Political Science Review*, vol. 9, 1988.

Rokkan, S. "Electoral Systems". In *International Encyclopedia of Social Sciences*. New York: Macmillan and Free Press, 1968.

Rose, J. F. *Elections and Electors*. London: Eyre and Spottiswood, 1955.

Rose, R. "Conclusion". In R. Rose and E. Suleiman (eds.), *Presidents and Prime Ministers*. Washingon DC: American Enterprise Institute, 1980.

Sager, S. *The Parliamentary System of Israel*. Syracuse, NY: Syracuse University Press, 1985.

Sartori, G. "The Party-Effects of Electoral Systems". In R. Hazan and M. Maor, "Parties, Elections and Cleavages: Israel in Comparative and Theoretical Perspective". Special Issue of *Israel Affairs*, vol. 6, Winter 1999.

—— "Neither Presidentialism nor Parliamentarism". In J. Linz and A. Valenzuela (eds.), *The Failure of Presidential Democracy*. Baltimore, MD: Johns Hopkins University Press, 1994.

—— "Political Development and Political Engineering". In J. D. Montgomery and A. O. Hirschman (eds.), *Public Policy*, vol. 17. Cambridge, MA: Harvard University Press, 1968.

—— "Representational Systems". In *International Encyclopedia of Social Sciences*, vol. 13. New York: Macmillan, 1968.

—— *Parties and Party Systems*. Cambridge: Cambridge University Press, 1976.

—— "European Political Parties: The Case of Polarized Pluralism". In J. LaPalombara and M. Weiner (eds.), *Political Parties and Political Development*. Princeton: Princeton University Press, 1966.

Schaffer, B. B. "The Concept of Preparation: Some Questions About the Transfer of Systems of Government". *World Politics*, vol. 8, October 1965.

Seliger, M. "Ideologia Ubechirot" [Idiology and elections], *Molad*, October 1960.

Shimshoni, D. *Israeli Democracy*. New York: Free Press, 1982.

Shofman, J. "Democratia Bemivcahn Bechirot" [The challenge of democratic elections]. *Ha'uma*, June 1963.

Bibliography

Shogan, R. *None of the Above: Why Presidents Fail and What Can Be Done About It*. New York and Scarborough, Ontario: New American Library, 1982.

Sternhal, Z. "Kvutzot Lachatz Ubechirot Rubiot" [Pressure groups and plurality systems]. *Ovnaim*, vol. 2, 1962.

Taagepera, R. and Shugart, R. M. *Seats and Votes: The Effects and Determinants of Electoral Systems*. New Haven and London: Yale University Press, 1989.

Van den Berg, G. *Shitot ha-behirot ba-olam* [Unity amongst diversity]. Jerusalem: Reuben Mas, 1959.

Vilnai, Z. *Atlas 1968: Shnat esrim li-medinat Yisrael* [Atlas 1968: Twenty years to the State of Israel]. Jerusalem: Jerusalem University Press, 1968.

Weinshel, A. "Bechirot Yachassiot o' Ezoriyot" [Proportional representation or a district system]. *Ha'uma*, vol. 20, 1969.

Wolfsohn, A. *Behirot azoriyot bi-Medinat Yisrael* [Constituency elections in the State of Israel]. Haifa: Halevanon, 1968.

Yaacobi, G. and Gera, E. *Hahofesh Livhor* [Freedom to choose]. Tel Aviv: Am Oved, 1975.

Yaacobi, G. *The Government* (Hebrew), second edn. Tel Aviv: Am Oved, 1980.

Zusser, B. (ed.). *The Political System of Israel* (in Hebrew). Tel Aviv: Bar Ilan University, 1987.

Index

Index

Barak, Ehud
  collapse of coalition (2001), 66, 91–2
  concessions to smaller parties, 70, 101
  elected (1999), 66, 71, 110
  maximum size of government, 67
  presidential system, 121*n*
Basic Law
  premier–parliamentary system, 65, 67, 110
  Section 4, 9–10
Bayliss, A. T., 71
Beersheba sub-district, 46, 49, 51, 52, 53, 54
Begin, Menachem, 60, 63, 91
Belgium, 34
Ben-Gurion, David
  departure from office (1953), 122*n*
  establishment of Rafi, 10
  simple-majority, single-ballot system, 9, 10, 16, 18, 62–3
  "status quo" agreement, 122*n*
Benelux, 14
bill of rights, 64
Birch, A. H., 75, 120*n*
Blondel, J., 122*n*
Bogdanor, Vernon, 15, 94
Britain
  ballot, 1
  basis of voter decisions, 7
  electoral district size, 1, 116*n*
  lack of independent candidates, 7
  premier–parliamentary system, 71
  simple-majority, single-ballot system, 20

cabinet, Israeli parliamentary system, 60, 89–90
Camp David Accords, 60
Center Party, Bi-Partisan Committee projection, 53
Central district, representation in the Knesset, 77, 78
charismatic leadership, 87
Citizens' Rights Movement (CRM), 17
civil service, 97
Coalition Committee on Electoral and Government Reform, 13, 17, 43–55, 58, 63–4
coalition governments, 87, 89–91, 97
  difficulty of establishing, 60–1
  durability of, 122*n*
  impact of electoral reform on, 102–3
  national versus local, 102–3
  premier–parliamentary system, 69–70, 84
  shortening of process of coalition formation, 72, 105

collective responsibility principle, 93
constituency-proportional system *see* proportional district representation
constituency-proportional system *see* proportional representation (PR) list system
constituency-proportional system *see* proportional subdistrict representation
Constituent Assembly, x, 9
"Constitution for Israel" movement, 95
Constitution, Law and Justice Committee
  Bi-Partisan Coalition Committee proposal, 13, 43, 44
  direct election of prime minister, 64
  electoral quotas, 16, 25, 50
  mixed proportional- constituency systems, 10, 12
  private member's bill, 63
constitutional change, 87, 94–5, 96
crises, 86–7
CRM *see* Citizens' Rights Movement (CRM)
Crotty, William J., 87
Czech Republic, electoral quota, 25

de Gaulle, Charles, 88, 94
Debré, Michel, 94
defense policies, 60, 90
Degel Hatora
  allocation of seats 10th to 15th Knesset, 4
  concessions to, 69
Democratic Arab Party, Bi-Partisan Committee projection, 53
Democratic Front for Peace and Equality (DFPE), allocation of seats 10th to 15th Knesset, 5
Democratic List for Peace
  allocation of seats 7th Knesset, 31
  proportional district representation projection, 31
Democratic Movement for Change (DMC), electoral reform, 11, 63
democratic tradition, 84–5
developmental towns, representation in the Knesset, 81
DFPE *see* Democratic Front for Peace and Equality (DFPE)
Diamond, L., 62
district size, 1–2
DMC *see* Democratic Movement for Change (DMC)
Dodd, C. L., 122*n*
domestic policies, 60, 90
Doron, G., 65

Index

High Court of Justice, 90
"highest-average" formula, 2–3
Holon sub-district, 46, 49, 51, 52, 53, 54
d'Hondt formula
    allocation of seats 10th to 15th Knesset,
        4–5
    Bi-Partisan Committee projection, 46–7,
        48, 49, 50, 51, 52, 53, 54, 55
    First Knesset, 23
    proportional subdistrict representation,
        16, 32–5, 36, 57
d'Hondt, Victor, 3, 48
Hurvitz, Yigal, 10, 16

Iceland, 121n
Independent Liberal Party
    allocation of seats 7th Knesset, 31
    proportional district representation
        projection, 31
    proportional subdistrict representation
        projection, 33, 35, 38
    Yaakobi proposal projection, 39, 40
inflation, 61
institution reforms, 85–9, 97
Israel Ba'aliya
    allocation of seats 10th to 15th Knesset, 5
    allocation of seats 14th Knesset, 69
    Bi-Partisan Committee projection, 53
    coalition partners, 70
    Ma'ariv poll, 111
Israel Communist Party, Yaakobi proposal
    projection, 39
Israel Labor Party, see also Alignment;
    Israel One; Labor Party
Israel One, 55, 69, 70
Israel Our Home, Bi-Partisan Committee
    projection, 53
Israel Workers' Party see Mapai
Italy, 35

Jerusalem district, 116n
    Bi-Partisan Committee projection, 46, 49,
        51, 52, 53, 54
    representation in the Knesset, 77, 78, 81
Jerusalem local council, 100, 105
Jews of the Bible Party, 26
Judea district
    Bi-Partisan Committee projection, 52, 54
    representation in the Knesset, 77, 78

Kach
    allocation of seats 10th to 15th Knesset, 4
    percentage of votes, 25

Kanzler system, x, xi, 71–2, 89, 110
kibbutz movement, 77, 78, 81
Kinneret sub-district see Safed & Kinneret
    sub-district
Knesset 1, 23
Knesset 2, 23
Knesset 6, proportional district representa-
    tion projection, 32
Knesset 7
    allocation of seats, 31
    proportional district representation
        projection, 30–1
    proportional subdistrict representation
        projection, 33–4, 35, 36, 37–8
    simple-majority system projection, 18–20
    two largest parties, 22
    Yaakobi proposal projection, 39–40
Knesset 8
    proportional subdistrict representation
        projection, 34, 35, 36, 38
    simple-majority system projection, 20–1,
        56
    two largest parties, 22
    Yaakobi proposal projection, 56
Knesset 10
    allocation of seats, 4–5
    simple-majority system projection, 22
Knesset 11
    allocation of seats, 4–5
    electoral quota projection, 25
    political party membership, 63
    proportional subdistrict representation
        projection, 36–7, 38
    simple-majority system projection, 22
    two largest parties, 22
Knesset 12
    allocation of seats, 4–5
    Bi-Partisan Committee projection, 46–7,
        48, 49, 51
    electoral quota projection, 25
    two largest parties, 22
Knesset 13
    allocation of seats, 4–5
    Bi-Partisan Committee projection, 50–5
    electoral quota projection, 25
Knesset 14
    allocation of seats, 4–5, 69
    Bi-Partisan Committee projection, 50, 54,
        55
    electoral quota projection, 25
Knesset 15
    allocation of seats, 4–5, 69

Index

Index

Index

Basic Law, 65, 67, 110
coalition governments, 69–70, 84
collective responsibility principle, 93
deficiencies of, 68–70, 84
and the Knesset, 65–8
presidential systems, xi, 84–98, 107–8
American, 71, 91–3
conceptual framework, 84–9
definition of, 68
French semi-presidential system, 59, 71,
85, 88, 93–4, 98, 121*n*
Israeli setting, 89–91
prime minister
constructive vote of no- confidence, 72,
105
direct election, xi, 27, 64–5, 66, 68–70,
88–9, 99–103
eligibility for candidacy, 66
powers of, 59–60, 67, 93–4
premier–parliamentary system, x, 65–70,
88–9, 93–4, 95, 102
Progressive List of Peace (PLP)
allocation of seats 10th to 15th Knesset, 5
percentage of votes, 25
Progressive Party
electoral quota, 23, 24
see also Independent Liberal Party
proportional district
representation, 27–32
electoral quotas, 27, 29, 108
Moab proposal, 17, 41–3, 58
Yaakobi proposal, 16–17, 38–41, 56,
57–8, 63
proportional representation (PR)
list system
Knesset, ix–x, 1–7, 95, 106–7
origins of, 8–9
strengths and weaknesses, 3–7
proportional subdistrict
representation
d'Hondt formula, 16, 32–5, 36, 57
Hare formula, 17, 35–8, 108
Public Committee for a Constitution for
Israel, 64

quasi-presidential systems, 85, 121*n*

Rabin, Yitzhak, 55, 60, 121*n*
Rae, Douglas, x, 14–15, 18, 56, 57
constituency sizes, 30, 31–2, 33
German plurality–proportionality
formula, 26
similarity of PR formulae, 35, 36
simple-majority system projection, 19–20
Rafi, 10

Rahat, G., 89
Rakah
allocation of seats 10th to 15th Knesset, 5
Bi-Partisan Committee projection, 46–7,
48, 49, 51
proportional subdistrict representation
projection, 33, 35, 37, 38
simple-majority system projection, 21, 22
Ramat Gan sub-district, 46, 49, 51, 52, 53,
54
Ramla-Rehovot sub-district, 46, 49, 51, 52,
53, 54
Ratz
allocation of seats 10th to 15th Knesset, 4
Bi-Partisan Committee projection, 46–7,
48, 49, 51
régime d'assemblée system, 59, 85, 86
regional representation, 6, 77, 78, 81
religious parties
allocation of seats 14th Knesset, 69
coalition partners, 65, 70, 89
Ma'ariv poll, 111
opposition to electoral reform, 64, 95, 97,
107–8
"status quo" agreement, 89–90
written constitution, 64
see also Agudat Yisrael; Degel Hatora;
Meimad Party; Morasha; National
Religious Party (NRP); Shas
religious sector
Likud bloc electoral support, 61
representation in the Knesset, 77, 82
see also Ultra-Orthodox Jews
representation
concept of, 73–6, 100
functions in politics, 74
in the Knesset, x–xi, 7, 76–83, 88
residential area, representation in the
Knesset, 77, 78, 82
rights, 85, 90
Rokkan, Stein, 14, 58
Rose, R., 91
Russia, electoral quota, 25

Safed & Kinneret sub-district
Bi-Partisan Committee projection, 46, 49,
51, 52, 53, 54
merger, 34
Saint Lague formula, 57
Samaria district
Bi-Partisan Committee projection, 52, 54
representation in the Knesset, 77, 78
Sartori, G., 59, 68, 71, 74, 108
Scandinavia, 14

145